FROM THE REVIEWS

"JAILBAIT is a book for the layman as well as the specialist. The text, although well documented, reads like an interesting novel . . . Bernard does get his point across that delinquency, in whatever form, is everybody's business."

San Francisco Chronicle

"All of us, at one time or another, have been appalled by stories of sexual orgies, juvenile murders, and various forms of crime, prostitution, and promiscuous activities committed by children and youths up to the age of 21. Some of us, unfortunately, have had direct contact with them. This is the story of those children, revealed simply and nakedly to the reader."

Rochester Democrat and Chronicle

"JAILBAIT is a valuable contribution to the growing list of publications on the vital problem of juvenile delinquency. It is a book well suited to the layman."

Brooklyn Eagle

"William Bernard's book will serve as an eye opener to many who would like to remain aloof to the affairs of their community. Covering the field of child crime and vice, JAILBAIT reports on gang degeneracy, schoolgirl scandals and teen-age rackets. The author does a good job of revealing traps and pitfalls which beset children and adolescents; he shows the maladjustments which, when neglected, lead youth into trouble."

Kansas City Star

"The author goes into intimate details of certain types of delinquency in an open and frank manner, showing the kinks of maladjustment, most of their causes and the criminal factors that aid young folks on their way."

Springfield Republican

Jailbait

**William
Bernard**

WILDSIDE PRESS

Author's Note

All case histories cited in these pages are authentic, though names, places, and other identifying characteristics are generally disguised.

The author wishes to acknowledge the co-operation of various Federal and state agencies, and to thank the many workers in the child welfare field who have given access to confidential material.

This book is dedicated: "To Davey W—, who made it all the way back."

1

Statistics of Sin

WHILE THE COPS WERE PULLING HER OUT OF THE prowl car, kicking and screaming like a hurt animal, 14-year-old Nanette tore her stockings. Her only nylons. Gossamer badges, in her own eyes, of freedom and adulthood. It didn't matter that her legs were too skinny to fill the things, that they curled and rolled limply around her adolescent thighs. She had worked for them, hard. With them to indicate professional status, to hint of cultivated technique and experience at collecting for same, she could now demand a dollar, even two. In fact, she had been busily embarked on her first venture at the new rates when members of the vice squad had so rudely broken into the hotel room.

"You can put her down now, officer," the desk sergeant said. "I've sent for a policewoman."

"Watch out for this kid!" The officer's wrist streamed blood where Nanette's nails had gashed deeply.

"You could have stopped to dress her."

"She threw everything but those stockings out the window. She was fixin' to jump after 'em, but I—"

"No guy?"

"Two. Both over fifty. Found one hiding in the shower bath. The other was . . . say, you'd be surprised! Had to let 'em go."

The desk sergeant wearily made notations and shooed
the cops out of the station room. Nanette's child-blue eyes
sought his.

"Put this on, kid." A heavy black police shirt supplanted
the ripped bedsheet wrapped around her. "How did you
get into the hotel?"

"Just walked upstairs. They told me their room number.
You don't think I'm dumb enough to use the elevator!"
Nanette's eyes returned to the torn stockings drooping over
her calves. A dollar and thirty-nine cents! She started to
cry.

Impulsively, the sergeant stepped down from his desk
to console the child. Nanette looked up at him. With desperate inspiration she slid an arm halfway around his sturdy
middle.

"Listen! For a dollar and thirty-nine cents, I'll—well,
anything—only a dollar thirty-nine—"

The sergeant had had a hard day. He felt a surge of
warm, guilty passion.

Then, more angry at himself than at the child, he slapped
her across the mouth. "You little slut!"

Nanette is a juvenile delinquent.

She stands for sin, but whose sin? Whose shame? No one
knows, exactly.

Experts disagree more than they agree concerning the
origins of delinquency. No man can say for sure who or
what is responsible for it.

But this much is certain. Forty thousand like Nanette
will go to reform schools this year.

Other hundreds of thousands will brush with the police,
be reprimanded, locked up, paroled, suspended, dismissed,
remanded in custody of parents, foster homes and sectarian
institutions.

That "hundreds of thousands" is pretty vague. Because
we simply do not know! We have exact enough information
on the bushels of wheat or tons of pig iron produced each
year, but the nation's crop of Nanettes is considered less
important. Its size has never been accurately calculated.

From the Children's Bureau of the Department of Labor comes the estimate that for every child delinquent who actually comes to the attention of the police, perhaps ten remain uncaught. Well, in a typical post-war year, roughly 100,000 delinquency cases are handled by juvenile courts reporting to the Children's Bureau. On this basis, the number of boys and girls annually guilty of delinquent behavior cannot be less than a million!

Now there are, between the ages of ten and eighteen, some twenty million Americans. Does this mean that one child in twenty is a delinquent? That one American child in twenty has committed a crime or definitely fallen below accepted minimum standards of conduct? No one has a reliable answer.

We are not even sure of the number arrested in any given year. "When we talk about children held in detention in the United States, we do not know what we are talking about . . . The only figures we have are estimates," says official Washington. And no accurate check on how many youngsters are in reform institutions has ever been made except once—in 1942, by the Connecticut Public Welfare Council. At that time, Connecticut held 76 children in such institutions for every 10,000 in the population. If, as the Children's Bureau surmises, ten young offenders go free for every one detected, does it follow that one child out of thirteen or fourteen in that state was a delinquent? We cannot be positive. The only thing certain is that as in Connecticut, so the country over. The amount of delinquency was then, and is now, frighteningly large—and growing larger.

One difficulty in getting precise knowledge of the delinquent lies in the lack of any central clearing house for information. Both the F.B.I. and the Children's Bureau try to fill the bill, but not all juvenile courts and police bureaus report to them. Nor do the reports observe uniform statistical standards. Some courts list truancy offenses, say, as delinquency; others do not. Many fail to report "unofficial" cases—delinquents helped without formal recourse to law, but *bona fide* delinquents just the same.

Further, confusion exists with respect to the terms them-

selves. Who is a "juvenile"? What is a "delinquent"? The
Connecticut survey and others characterize as *juvenile* any
boy or girl up to twenty-one. This book does likewise, though
emphasis shall be on boys below eighteen and girls below
seventeen. As for *delinquency,* some authorities use it to
cover only offenses actually recorded by police or courts.
Others include minor misbehaviors with which no self-
respecting policeman would ordinarily be bothered, such
as tieing a can to Fido's tail or stealing candy from a baby.
Here the word shall be used to refer both to offenses causing
action by police, court or welfare authorities—and those
which *would* cause such action were they detected.

In general, people sense accurately enough the meaning
of "juvenile delinquent"; broadly it applies to any boy or
girl who gets "in trouble." But it must be borne in mind
that "delinquency" is only a nicer word for crime, for transgression against society.

Juvenile delinquents have always been with us. They have
been with all societies. But the problem did not seem to
reach really alarming proportions in the United States until
the beginning of World War II.

Up to 1939 there had been hope that we were successfully
coping with delinquency. But at that time the slow down-
ward trend of the previous decade sharply reversed itself.
By 1943, all the barriers and defenses against child crime
so painfully developed over the years seemed to have utterly
broken down. Delinquency leaped forty percent above the
ten-year pre-war average, and in many localities soared
even higher than that. J. Edgar Hoover of the F.B.I. pro-
claimed, "It is approaching a national scandal."

During the first nine months of 1943, arrests of children
aged seventeen and younger rose twenty percent over the
same period of 1942, itself a peak year. In 1944, according
to the Federal Security Agency, 78 juvenile courts in communities of 100,000 or more alone handled nearly 90,000
cases!

Those were the years, you remember, when San Diego

reported delinquency up 50 percent for boys, 355 percent
for girls. Indianapolis court officials publicly confessed panic
before the rising tide of delinquency; Atlanta magistrates
nervously advised calm. Cleveland, Norfolk, Brooklyn and
Pendleton, Ore., were among the cities reporting murders
by schoolkids. Arson flamed across the country, destroying
a munitions plant in New Jersey and movie theaters in
California; the F.B.I. complained of more trouble from
juvenile saboteurs than from enemy spies! Students at a
famous old New England school launched a crime wave
of their own, stealing railroad tickets and then riding to
various towns to pillage and pilfer. Miami and Boston led
a hundred other cities in setting up special police squads
just to handle child crime. Great gangs of kids waged war
on the streets of Washington, Los Angeles, San Antonio,
St. Louis, Kansas City, Philadelphia, New York. Congress
began an investigation.

Particularly disturbing was the rise in offenses among
girls—nearly doubled, according to local authorities and
the F.B.I., in those categories covering vagrancy, drunkenness, disorderly conduct, prostitution and sexual waywardness of all kinds. "Victory Girls" sold themselves for small
change to any uniform. In Portland, the Union Depot
swarmed with 12-year-old girls offering themselves to sailors;
in Indianapolis and Cleveland the bus and railroad stations
blossomed with 15- and 16-year-olds as anxious to accommodate soldiers. From Sacramento to Detroit, from Seattle
to Mobile, teen-agers solicited in drugstores over their
malted milks. The great ports of embarkation crawled with
giggling semipros in bobby-sox; Manhattan's Central Park,
San Francisco's notorious Turk Street, Chicago's Michigan
Avenue, all reeked of precocious sex.

Civilian lads, too young for the services, held orgies when
and where they could find girls; typically, in the box of one
Bronx theater a girl of seventeen was raped by eight boys.
And the hysteria seeped down, with crime appearing, so
to speak, in diapers. A 6-year-old Philadelphia child crawled
under movie seats to open purses, giving himself away by
flashing large bills before a pair of 5-year-old girl friends.

Children from nine to fourteen derailed trains in Pennsylvania, New York, Maryland . . .

All over the country makeshift local remedies were tried in vain, until Magistrate Mark Rhoads of Indianapolis Juvenile Court publicly despaired: "The hell with the future—that seems to be our philosophy. Definitely the problem has grown too large for us to handle adequately!"

How right he was . . .

In 1943, the "future" was 1948. And in 1948 not fewer than 759,698 persons were arrested and fingerprinted. The predominating age of these major violators, according to the F.B.I.? Twenty-one!

These hardened 21-year-old criminals were the juvenile delinquents of 1943. Thus we reap the whirlwind.

Is the situation getting any better?

Everyone assumed during the war that "morals" were bound to slide. The restraints were off! Things will improve, we said, when peace comes. And in 1946, the first full postwar year, this prediction seemed justified. Two hundred and twenty juvenile courts reported a continuation of the slight drop which had appeared immediately after the war's end. The F.B.I. also reported a decrease that year in arrests of girls under twenty-one.

But the number still exceeded the pre-war average by forty percent! And while juvenile crime as a whole had decreased somewhat in frequency as compared to the year before, it showed a trend to the graver and more violent offenses.

Judge for yourself. The F.B.I., in 1946, announced a ten-year peak for American crime—with a major offense occurring every 18.7 seconds around the clock. Compared with the previous year, murders were up 23 percent; rape, 5 percent; burglaries, 11 percent. "The juvenile delinquents of the war years," said J. Edgar Hoover, "are graduating from petty thieves to armed robbers and into the field of more serious crime."

In 1948, "serious crime" maintained its pace, with an

over-all increase of nearly five percent over 1947. Each day averaged 36 persons slain—463 autos stolen—1032 places burglarized—200 victims assaulted or raped. In larger cities, as compared with the pre-war average from 1918 to 1941, rapes were up 50 percent; burglaries, 17 percent; murders, 14 percent. New York City alone hung up this tally: 315 murders and non-negligent manslaughters, 1515 robberies, 2810 rapes and assaults, 2726 burglaries, 7713 larcenies, 10,091 automobile thefts!

Remember, the "predominating" age of those committing these major offenses was twenty-one years. All too often today's delinquent grows into tomorrow's hardened criminal. Juvenile delinquency is not only a grave problem in itself, but root and father to a graver one.

And while one or two of the post-war years have shown slight regressions, again child crime is dangerously on the upswing. In 1948 and the first six months of 1949 it appeared to exceed pre-war levels by a solid fifty percent. Further, the youngest group of offenders, those below the age of fourteen, once more is showing the increases characteristic of the war period, exceeding the old averages by from five to thirty percent in cities across the country.

These younger delinquents of today are a strange, cold crew, often vicious where their predecessors were merely adventurous. One Child Guidance Bureau psychiatric worker in New York attributes their rise to the same social upheavals which spawned so many child offenders during the war. "Those disturbances also affected parents, and through them were passed on to the crop of infants at the time. Now the infants have matured, with the disturbances ripening into delinquent behavior."

With the growth of these saplings, delinquency seems again to be climbing on every police graph. Definitive figures are lacking, but the trend is unmistakable. Child-gang warfare flourishes in our big cities and some of the smaller ones. Again newspapers and national magazines are running sensational articles on the sins and vices of youth. Alarmed warnings come from pulpits; courts and welfare departments from coast to coast plead for greater public efforts to stem the growing scourge. And one New York police official sadly shakes his head as he tells the press, "It was bad enough during the war—but we've never seen anything like this!"

What is the answer? No single or absolute solution exists. Some of the many approaches to prevention and cure shall be discussed later, but all involve consideration of the various types and manifestations of delinquency. So first, let us look straight into the face of this most vexatious and potentially dangerous of modern social problems.

For if it is a wise father that knows his own child, it is also a wise country that knows its own juveniles

2

The Juvenile Prostitute

A MAGISTRATE OF NEW YORK'S ADOLESCENT COURT, not easily shocked after years of probing into every sort of juvenile depravity, listened open-mouthed to the unfolding of a story of a ring of "call girls"—aged 12 to 14! Six of the girls stood shamefaced in court. Twenty-five others remained to be arrested. Fifty men were to be arraigned on charges of statutory rape, most of them between 50 and 60 years old.

What hardened procurer had trafficked thus heartlessly in the bodies and souls of schoolgirls?

Detectives brought the culprit before the court. Redheaded, five feet tall, weighing less than a hundred pounds, she stood cool and poised in pink sweater, green slacks and white playshoes, playing with a gold bracelet as she chatted easily with the matron. Her name was Carol. She was barely seventeen.

Two years before, she had organized her "ring"—an accomplished and efficient "madam" at fifteen!

Yes, at that tender age the enterprising Carol had rounded up a few girls willing to visit men—mostly elderly Latins in the slum neighborhood around Rivington Street. Soon she had a full stable of adolescents who, after school or on week ends, became the youngest apprentices to the oldest profession. There was no street-walking or anything like that. Carol made the appointments. She would meet each girl and personally conduct her to the store or apartment of the customer. There she would collect in advance, usually keeping half the money and giving the rest to the girl. Sometimes customers would require a place of assignation. Carol made an arrangement with the proprietor of a store on Twenty-first Street. She paid him a half-dollar for each customer entertained in the rear room of his establishment—a sum she took not from her own share, of course, but from that of the assigned girl.

Carol kept her kids busy. Some testified that they entertained three or four men a night. "Carol would get from $1.50 to $2 each, and pay us out of that," explained one 14-year-old pupil at P.S. 60, on Twelfth Street. This girl had been picked up on returning home from a schedule so heavy that she had been missing three days.

One girl complained that Carol "paid off in quarters." Yet the tip-off on the ring, after two years of successful operation, came when teachers noticed that certain girls were attending classes with pockets literally bulging with money. In a slum neighborhood, this was enough to arouse suspicion. The school called the Children's Aid Society, which in turn called the police.

All concerned with the case were dumfounded, yet could not conceal a certain admiration for Carol's skill and energy. She took care of her girls with technical advice and, when they were old enough to need them, with contraceptives. She watched out for venereal symptoms, and sometimes treated them herself. She worked hard, neglecting no details except, perhaps, income tax. Such ability, everyone agreed, if turned to legitimate pursuits, would have made Carol an outstanding success!

At the final hearing, less than a month after her arrest, all charges against Carol were withdrawn. She was adjudged a wayward minor, suitable for rehabilitation. Her mother scrawled an "X" on certain legal documents, and Carol was committed for an indefinite period to a training institution conducted by a religious organization. The judge, with that optimism which all must have who work with adolescents, told the schoolgirl offender:

"It is to your best interest, and to society's . . . Everyone wants to help you . . . You will be among friends . . . You can be made into a useful woman . . . Forget the past and look brightly on your future. . . ."

But when Carol is released, what then? Will a girl of her obvious ambition, nerve and initiative be content to remain in some factory or sales job—even if, with her record, she can find one? Or will she find herself slipping back into the pandering industry? After all, how else can a poverty-stricken, unschooled slum lass, stated in court to be the "sole support of her family," ever get to wear gold bracelets?

To understand delinquency, we must break it into its parts and examine them separately. For "delinquency," like "disease," is a categorical term. Just as pneumonia will show neither the same symptoms nor the same origins as yellow fever, so with the various forms of delinquency. Prostitution—gangsterism—truancy—such groupings are admittedly amorphous, impinging one on the other, yet each has its own characteristics. And may require, possibly, its own cures.

Our classification begins with Carol's case. It illustrates child prostitution—that category of delinquency which probably most stirs popular indignation and causes judicial eyebrows to be lifted highest.

On the heels of Carol's trial, a similar syndicate of child prostitutes serving elderly customers was broken up in Newark, N. J. Since then, other rings of 12- to 15-year-olds have fallen to the law in all parts of the country.

Unfortunately, the demand for Carol's sort of merchandise shall persist. To what extent males, especially elderly males, feel the urge to cohabit with girls below the age of consent is unknown. But the constant recurrence of versions of the story indicates that it is a stubborn one. Classical and modern literature, as well as the daily newspapers, are full of instances, incestuous and otherwise.

Various cultures even today countenance the outright sale of children for purposes of prostitution, and find nothing amiss in marriage of girls of 14 or younger. In the United States, however, adult-child intercourse out of wedlock is held highly reprehensible, and in a majority of states prohibited even within wedlock. We may accept this as right and proper. The moral issue involved is not so much that in itself the thing is sinful, as that too early an introduction to sex may inhibit the social, ethical and even physical development of the individual. Of course, this view has been rather sharply criticized in recent years with growing recognition of the sex needs of young people and alarm at possible damage due to sex repression. But even those who take this advanced stand seldom deny that when prostitution is involved—when young bodies are bartered for money or other goods—the child is being deeply injured, at least ethically.

Hence the public shock when a girl sells herself, its intensity varying inversely with her years.

Fortunately, exploitation of children by adult procurers is not common in this country. Most sex involvements of even criminal adults with adolescents are dictated by the passions, not by profit motives. Definitely a certain squeamishness in this respect exists among the worst as among the best of us.

Occasionally an adult does turn up who has a stronger stomach than the rest of the world. About the time of the Carol affair, for example, a heavily rouged procuress of forty-seven years was arraigned for soliciting in the streets for a number of schoolgirl prostitutes. But the case is not typical. Organized vice does not go in for child labor. Even the fringe enterprises leave it alone, for it simply is not profitable: the kind of man who keeps the brothel busy wants more for his money than a skinny schoolkid. And the kind of roué who wants a skinny schoolkid generally does his own promoting—as we shall see. As adolescents approach the age of consent, of course, they become more interesting as prey for organized vice; yet here it is difficult to distinguish, except in a legal sense, between woman and juvenile. More important as a threat to juvenile morals, probably, is a certain type of enterprise which does not sell sex as such, but uses it as a blandishment.

We refer to roadhouses, night clubs and "bebop" joints which infest every town and highway, whose main attraction is the strip-tease. Minors are not officially admitted—yet often enough they cram these places. Here under the influence of liquor and nudity-inflamed importunities, many a girl has yielded to the ultimate push of a ten-dollar bill.

There are also "businesses" which make attractive offers to unwary adolescents, including the bait of "traveling expenses," and after luring them from their homes make capital of their charms.

One 17-year-old girl from Houston, an engaging and husky blonde, did not seem to mind. She had arrived in St. Louis so penniless that she offered, in a bar, to exchange her embraces for a place to spend the night. She told the man she approached—who happened to be a city detective —"It was good while it lasted. We sold ties and things from door to door around colleges, and whenever we got a couple of fellows alone, we made a big sale, you bet. I got to be crew manager. The boss died, but I'm going to start my own business—as soon as I get together a little money."

Other girls, when caught up in such rackets, strenuously object. As in the case of Dora.

Her boss, an elegant dresser of forty-six, one day found himself held for $15,000 bail at General Sessions Court. The charge was coercion of twenty pretty girls into prostitution. Their ages ran from seventeen to twenty-three. There was reason to believe that many had falsified their ages in order to get the job; certainly they looked younger than they professed to be. These girls had been hired as "solicitors for magazine subscriptions." Dora told newspaper reporters this story:

She had noticed an advertisement in her local paper asking for young ladies "willing to travel to California with a chaperone." Expense money and a drawing account were mentioned. She answered the ad, and during the interview was queried as to whether she would be required to return home by a specific date, whether she had any close ties, whether she had family assistance or was really dependent on a job. Out of six candidates that day, she alone was hired. Introduced to a man called only "the boss," she found herself installed in a hotel and was told to sell subscriptions to magazines.

The girl objected that she lacked experience. He instructed her that the best way to sell was to stop people on the street, particularly servicemen, and "finger" them. "That is—I was to run my hand over their face, chin, chest or any other part of their bodies to make them stop and listen to me . . . When I went out the first day, I don't remember whether I sold any subscriptions or not. I just couldn't bring myself to use his methods."

After two or three days he assigned another girl to work with her and smarten her up. The girl advised Dora to leave town and go home.

She was ashamed to. She didn't want to return a failure.

"After a while," Dora said, "I did make some sales. The boss asked me to his room. He complimented me on my progress and told me a lot of things I don't ever want to remember. Then . . ."

Then: the boss informed her that when subscription sales were not up to a certain mark, the best thing to do was to sell herself, charging as much as she could get. The proceeds were to go half to her, half to him—a split similar to that of the subscription deal. Either way, she would have to turn in a certain amount each day.

When she did not live up to this "quota," she was fined.

Dora continued: "Many times, to prevent my leaving town, he would leave me with just a bit of money. I was almost always in debt. A couple of times I couldn't pay my hotel bills and he'd move me to another place. He told me the first hotel was holding my clothes as security, but I learned later he had paid the bill and kept my clothing. He always saw to it that I had only one or two dresses so I wouldn't try to leave the city.

"Sometimes he'd accuse me of holding out on him. If I came in late for work he'd fine me five dollars or more. There was a time when I thought he owed me around forty dollars. When I told him so, he said he had fined me for coming in late one morning and had forgotten to tell me about it."

After a while Dora got up the courage to announce to the boss that she was quitting. "He became very angry and hit me." She was beaten on other occasions, too, as on the evening she had entertained some musicians and had brought back too little money.

"When he saw I was really leaving," she went on, "he accused me of giving someone venereal disease. He threatened me by saying he could prove it and make trouble for me.

"Later I found out I wasn't diseased. As a matter of fact, of all the girls working for him I think only two were infected."

Dora's release from her boss came only after he was arrested.

Here the lure of being "away from home," "on her own," led a girl to accept a condition little better than slavery.

Still another kind of enterprise, though not organizing child vice per se, sometimes acts as a focal point and center of encouragement, and at any rate draws benefit from the traffic. Coming under this head are the unscrupulous "tourist camps," and hotels, or employes of such places who procure as an avocation. Tourist camps are almost impossible to control in this respect, as they do no more on the face of it than sell legitimate accommodations. It is not theirs to go deeply into the ages or other circumstances of couples supplied with beds, and in this country people are not required to show passports, police cards, marriage licenses, birth certificates and similar papers to secure lodgings. Besides, your tourist camp collects no bonus, no direct wages of sin. With offending hotels, however, the situation is often quite different.

In one large city, for example, three justices sit down to try three prominent hotel men, each operating a separate establishment, on charges of running bawdy houses. The hotels are not hideaways or dives, but large, well-known enterprises in the busiest part of town. Seventeen-year-old Camille testifies to daily entertainment of men. One of many such girls, she began registering at one or another of the hotels at the age of sixteen. Bellboys steered clients to her, for a share of the five to twenty dollars she collected from each visitor. Some of the money taken by the bellboys found its way to the management or higher employes.

Here is a more detailed account of one such girl, bringing out several points. First, suburban juveniles as well as city ones can find their way into organized prostitution. Second, it can be difficult for a young girl to work as an independent. Third, a hotel, in any case, comes in handy. The following is paraphrased from two lengthy reports of juvenile court workers:

Jean's parents were divorced before she was 10. Her father considered her mother "loose," and Jean never heard from her after the divorce. The father sent Jean to live with her grandparents in a comfortable suburb in a neighboring state, not much different from her former home. Her father married again, moved to a distant city. At 12, Jean ran away from her grandparents' home. Picked up and brought back, she ran away twice more, each time being returned by police. She claimed that she wanted to look for her mother and father.

The grandparents were average people, and did not put unusual restrictions on Jean. There is evidence that at the age of 14 she was seduced by a village boy in the fields. Far from feeling shame, this exhilarated her, and her desires for independence were strengthened. She ran away again. She looked older than her age, and got a job as a waitress after hitch-hiking hundreds of miles. When 15, she was approached by a man who promised plenty of money, fine clothes, easy life, etc. He transported her across a state line to a brothel. By this time she had had several sex experiences, and did not object.

On the first night of her employment, Jean served seven men. The following night she was assigned to a different house, but the management took most of her earnings, reported at $30 to $40 per night. Convinced there was no future in the brothel, she decided to prostitute on her own.

At 16, Jean became discouraged by unstable returns, fatigue, police restrictions on soliciting. She was quite ready to give up her "independence" for comfort and convenience. She made contact with a hotel, with whose call girls she had been competing. She also registered at another hotel, where she kept up an appearance of respectability, doing all work at the first hotel only. Youth and looks brought her many calls from the latter's highly transient clientele, steered to her through bellboys. . . .

At about this time, police raided a much smaller hotel of only sixty rooms at a nearby address, and discovered twenty unregistered girls. They also discovered the surprising fact that some rooms were being rented out four and five times a night.

Goaded by public indignation, the police next raided Jean's hotel. That was how Jean came to be picked up. When arrested, she was seventeen, had little money, and suffered from a venereal infection. In the course of the trial, a chambermaid testified that Jean was one of a hundred girls similarly available to keep the hotel's clientele happy, not to mention the penicillin industry. The proceedings against the hotel brought out that the management derived profit, over and above regular room rent, from the traffic. According to Jean's testimony, she received up to twenty dollars from each client. The latter, in addition, paid for the hotel room at twice the regular rates. Out of every five dollars she collected, she paid two to the bellhop who had referred the customer. The bellhop captain, whose salary was a nominal "$1.14 per week," testified that deals with prostitutes were so profitable that boys were required to pay the management about fifteen dollars a day for the concession—a fee that was doubled during the busy seasons!

The proceedings led to the arrest and conviction of the man who first had delivered the young Jean to a brothel. Sentencing him, the judge said: "You simply are no good. You have no moral concepts. The only fit place for you is behind prison bars."

Did Jean, by this time, have moral concepts?

Only one stark fact need be mentioned to indicate the degree to which she had absorbed her particular education.

While she was being held pending disposition, she made immoral propositions to her fellow prisoners.

However, Jean had cooperated with police and the prosecuting authority. In the hope that she would return to rectitude, she was handed over to her father. He, at this late date, undertook to reconstruct her social outlook in a place far removed from the scenes of her delinquency. It was thought possible that an affectionate relationship with her father and stepmother might serve to reorient Jean.

Within two weeks, the father felt obliged to report that Jean was beyond his control; she kept irregular hours and consorted suspiciously with men. Soon after, Jean was again apprehended and, now a young woman, sentenced to a reformatory.

Concerning individual or unorganized child prostitution, little can be generalized. Instances are so numerous and so widely encountered in common experience that they need not be labored by itemization here. It has been woman's privilege, since Eve, to trade on her attractions—if not for money, then for security, social position and other rewards great or trifling, including psychological ones. How far the trade may be carried, and at what age it may start, is not only a matter of individual idiosyncrasy but also of general custom. Is a child considered delinquent if she accepts a candy bar in exchange for a pat on the head from that nice old man? No. If she accepts a ball for a kiss? Hardly. A quarter, after she sits on his lap? Well—maybe. A dollar for going to his apartment with him? Definitely!

It is widely accepted that juvenile prostitutes emerge from homes of generally poor morality, and of desperate need. So they do. No one questioned counsel's statement in behalf of young Carol that "the environment was not conducive to proper conduct." But what of the dismaying myriad of cases marked by juvenile sex participation where the environment *is* conducive to proper conduct?

At this point, enter the villain. It takes two to make sexual traffic. Or a recruit to prostitution. What chance has the nice, unsuspicious, unknowing child against the fatherly male skilled in seduction? How is the virginal schoolgirl to interpret his tenderness as something more than friendship?

The technique is old, and so, generally, are its practitioners. Usually it goes something like this: the lecherous Lothario accidentally encounters a young girl on her way home from school. He can ask her to help him across a street, to carry a package for him, to take him home, perhaps, because he is not feeling well. He may have a highly respectable address. If his invitation fails the first time, he will try again later, after a number of encounters in the street have made the two nodding acquaintances. The sequel nearly always is the same. He will at once create an image of himself that cries out for pity. He is lonely. The girl reminds him of his niece, or his poor, deceased daughter. If only she would visit him sometimes! He offers her gifts. He is so grateful. Obviously, he really is lonely, and in need of kindness. What else is a decent—and quite flattered—child to think?

This line of attack, so often successful even with mature women, on the record has betrayed many a childish trust. The girl returns to visit him. There is desultory conversation. Sweets are served. The old man establishes the habit of a parting paternal kiss. Of course, he has sworn her to secrecy. He will visit her parents some time, in the future, but right now it is she in whom he is interested. Others might not understand, he explains, and the girl nods thrilled assent to the conspiracy. He takes to giving her money. His kiss becomes warmer. If she feels embarrassed at the growing ardor of his embrace, she explains it away as part of his devotion. If she objects, he attributes it merely to his warm affection. Then at some propitious time he may persuade her to taste wine in honor of, say, his birthday. But with or without stimulant, he will prey upon any girl's normal proclivity to, and interest in, sexual excitation. Pleasure, or more tangible rewards, encourage her to repeat her visits.

The denouement? Complete or partial capitulation. Or,

with girls of tougher fiber, sudden defeat for the Casanova.

But, in the case of the failure, the very fear or shame which blocked capitulation serves as assurance that the child will not reveal the offender. She blushes at the thought of what people would think—if ever they should learn of the dangers she courted. And the non-failures? Until the rake tires of them, they collect money or other satisfactions. Then he passes them on to new benefactors—or they must seek their own.

This narrative of seduction is standard. Thus, on occasion, are our daughters trapped into prostitution, or in those cases where monetary reward is not the prime motivating factor, something resembling it. The calling may or may not be carried on in later life.

Differing considerably is the kind of free-lancing so popular during the war. The "Victory Girl" craze which saw thousands of girls of 12 to 16 years throwing themselves at uniformed boys has never been adequately explained. Patriotism? Why didn't the kids just sell bonds? Financial reward? Not at those prices—and besides, most families were relatively well off! Well, could it be that the kids really didn't have families, with home life as disturbed as it was? Unquestionably this played its part in provoking the hysteria. And what about excitement, adventure? These too, we believe, furnished a main motive.

But looking back at the pinched girls, the tawdry finery, the often pathetic stories, we can glimpse something else in the causation pattern. One underlying characteristic featured a surprising number, probably a majority, of the cases: the chief satisfaction they were getting from their escapades was simply—fellowship! It was as if their families had failed them in filling their needs for affection. So, by lending their bodies, they created an atmosphere of affection, if only a transient and spurious one. They were wanted, needed, made much of—at least for a moment.

Victory Girls are no longer with us. Does today's lass who gives herself to boys in the neighborhood, with roof or cellar for a setting and a few cents for reward, display any similar pattern of craving for fellowship and affection?

Study of case histories shows that she does. Every welfare worker knows the drab girl whose eyes light up as she recounts her crimson adventures. In each one, some boy wants her, perhaps desperately. Neighborhood lads seek her out, chase her, compete for her. If they can't give her money, they give her what they can, maybe a nice walk in the park or a bus ride uptown. "Nobody bothers about me at home. In school I'm in the dumb class." How different when panting Johnny strokes her, kisses her, enjoys her . . . in short, loves her.

When all is said and done, then, three basic considerations emerge from our brief investigation of prostitutional delinquency.

First: in the words of Dr. Karen Horney, "The neurotic need for affection often takes the form of a sexual infatuation or an insatiable hunger for sexual gratification." Parents who fear for their daughters would do well to ply them with tenderness and care, rather than preachings.

Second: where desperate need exists, desperate measures result. A girl hungry for money, adornment or simple excitement is not always amenable to moral argument. Especially when she lives in an environment characterized by jungle law.

Third: until the gap between public morality and private behavior grows less, juvenile prostitution in more or less degree must continue to exist. It is not just that hypocrisy sets a bad example for youngsters. Nor that a relative handful of elderly rakes act as recruiting-sergeants for the profession. The fact is that if there were no customers, there would be no child prostitutes!

3

School Scandal

MOST OF US HAVE A TOUCHING FAITH THAT OUR children are pretty safe at school. And so, in the main, they are. Supervision and inspection are almost always adequate to root out the grosser evil influences which might "impair the morals" of school children.

Yet anybody who reads the newspapers must notice disquieting things. Tales of rowdyism and vandalism appear with almost monotonous regularity. Occasionally more sinister stories crop up of school gangs tyrannizing smaller children through miniatures of the same techniques made famous by adult "mobs"—techniques for which perfect manuals are widely available in news stories, comic books, movies. And once in a while reporters unearth a nest of sexual misbehavior.

Such reports point up the stubborn persistence of a second major type of delinquency—delinquency occurring in, or associated with, the schools.

Ask yourself how often you have seen such newspaper items as this:

> . . . Brooklyn high school students may be denied customary free admittance to Dodger home games in Ebbets Field. Associate Supt. Ernst has received complaints that on each of five occasions this year high school students did not conduct themselves properly . . .
> —*N. Y. Post, May 26, 1949*

The complaints specified "noisy conduct, foul language and breaking of seats." This is a case of rowdyism. Only a couple of days before, one of the more common kinds of school vandalism had been reported.

Police of Stagg St. station were pained to learn that vandals had got into P.S. 36, half a block away and across the street, and made a shambles of nineteen classrooms.

The cops hadn't seen or heard a thing—although the marauders must have made enough noise for an old-fashioned Fourth of July celebration. The exuberant pranksters not only had made merry with books, papers, ink, and paints but had smashed desks, chairs and benches, shattered window panes and heaved some of the broken equipment out of the windows.

—*N. Y. Daily News, May 24, 1949*

Mark Barth, the school principal, said that his "was not a tough neighborhood," and somewhat plaintively complained that he couldn't understand it; nothing of the kind had happened before during his twenty-three years as principal. One cop offered this solution: "Probably the kids were tired of looking at the seventy-year-old building."

This hoodlum misbehavior, though troublesome and often vicious enough, is not the true stuff of delinquency. Often it is mere expression of exuberance, of simple "gross motor activity," on the part of unmannerly youngsters "showing off" to each other. Have we not all seen infants play quietly with a toy for some time, then suddenly throw it on the floor and begin stamping on it violently, at the same time uttering loud noises indicating great glee?

Even the occasional misconduct of schoolmaster or schoolmarm with girl or boy pupil, as sometimes reported in the press, signifies no special school reprehensibility. A certain amount of aberration must be expected when millions of individuals are thrown into daily contact. In every large group there are those who cannot withstand the temptations.

But the really disturbing goings-on are not often mentioned. Genuinely tainted schools, those contaminating children and adolescents, do not generally make the papers even when known to teachers and case workers. This is due in part to the latter's reticence about publicizing professional inadequacies—along with hesitation to uncover situations reflecting on superiors who can make things unpleasant for the tattler. There is proper zeal, too, in avoiding any stigma which might become publicly attached to a child. Of course, immorality-shot conditions in the schools are infrequent—relatively infrequent, that is. But shocking cesspools of iniquity do exist, usually in quieter corners. And some, not quietly hidden at all, brazenly foul whole school districts.

One example notorious in the professional literature is a high school for girls in a great eastern city.

Built to accommodate 2,000 pupils, it has a current attendance of some 4,600.

It stands in a neighborhood once rather upper-crust, and which, while gone to seed for a good many years, is not yet quite a slum district. The location is near one of those sharp lines of demarcation suddenly occurring in large cities; to the north runs a large Negro population, to the south, a white one. Students are chiefly Negro, but with a good admixture of whites of Latin parentage.

Delinquency in all its forms is supposed to run rampant in the classrooms, corridors and particularly the washrooms. Yet, on examination, most of this boils down to wilful mischief—to minor quarrels and feuds among various stocks and color segments—to inevitable disharmonies resulting from crowding, the tenseness of overworked teachers, the disturbances carrying over from teeming streets. One major type of delinquency flourishes, however. Sexual misconduct.

How ingrained this has become at R—— High School may be judged from the fact that many of those best acquainted with the situation believe it to be virtually impossible to root out. Teachers and welfare workers, grown accustomed to it over the years, are inclined to take it for granted. It has become traditional, like the daisy chain at Vassar. While police and Board of Education information is kept pretty secret, the author was kindly permitted an off-the-record glimpse at a few of the case histories compiled by a private welfare group. Here is an excerpt:

Celia, 16, native white extraction, general health good except for myopic condition. Refuses glasses. Grades fair.

Very strong. Excels in gymnasium. Religious upbringing. Queried on complaints of other girls, replied: "Why pick on me? I got it when I was a freshman, now I'm dishing it out. Doesn't hurt anybody." Not shy of boys, according to mother, but directs sex play at girls only.

The author was able to accompany a volunteer worker for one of the Negro welfare groups, visiting a girl stubbornly truant. She had reason to be. Slim and well-formed, stockingless but otherwise neatly dressed, she answered questions with angry frankness:

INVESTIGATOR: You used to like school, Mae. Why, you're very bright. Tenth grade at fourteen!

CHILD: I won't go, no. How can I go?

INVESTIGATOR: You mean because of what happened? Mrs. ——— (principal) told me. . . . Something in the gym, was it? Oh, yes, the washroom—

CHILD: Why doesn't she tell it over the radio?

INVESTIGATOR: Don't feel that way. No reason for you to feel ashamed, Mae. Sometimes things happen—

CHILD: This was the second time. The first time they just grabbed me and tickled me. All over. I bit one—that Sarah—

INVESTIGATOR: When was this? The same girls?

CHILD: About—last month, some time. These were different kids. They said they would initiate me into their bunch. They took my dress off and made me walk up and down. They were laughing and kissing me. They were feeling each other and laughing and touching me. Two were hugging on the floor, sort of, and they—

INVESTIGATOR: How many were there?

CHILD: Five—well, six, I think. They were from gym class. So I was fighting, but one took down her bloomers and they made me—

INVESTIGATOR: Why didn't you scream?

CHILD: They would of killed me, man! They said to keep my mouth shut or they'd kill me. They knew Mr. ——— (on corridor duty) couldn't come in. He must of heard

something or somebody snitched, he called Miss ———.
So she ran in and everybody ran away. She said to me:
"Get dressed, what's the matter with you?" and she took
me to the office.

INVESTIGATOR: Look, Mae, we've sent Gussie away. Elaine,
too. We'll get after Sarah. You don't have to worry. It
won't happen again.

CHILD: Man, I won't go back, no!

INVESTIGATOR: I tell you what. We'll get you transferred to
another school.

CHILD: I won't go, no. I'm afraid. (Crying) I won't go.

These cases are typical of dozens and perhaps hundreds,
many wholly unprintable, on the record cards of city and
private case workers. Despite all that school authorities can
do, the condition persists from year to year. "Before the war
we had a lot of pilfering and other stuff, too," a school official
told the author. "Most of that has died down here. Even this
vice is beginning to fall off. There's a better organized community effort to combat delinquency, and it's showing
results." He added, "I think things generally began to improve the day they appointed more Negro teachers to the
school."

"But sexual irregularity persists?"

"Well, less of it. It's quieter, less overt."

"How much of the school is exposed to this sort of thing?"

"I've heard guesses that as many as one in ten of the student body come in contact with it. Three to four per cent
would be nearer correct, I would say."

"To what do you attribute it?"

"The whole moral tone of the area is low. Sometimes you
see men in the streets, maybe in cars, waiting to pick up girls
after school. Did you know that two dope peddlers were
caught near the entrances this year? Marijuana."

The "tone" of the area might indeed be "low." Yet here
as in the best neighborhoods a great majority of the youngsters are perfectly nice kids. The tragedy lies in the exposure
of such children to humiliation, sexual terrorism and plain
seduction into "bad" ways. Where is their protection?

Nor is the institution in question unique. What a careful city-to-city survey would reveal is anybody's guess, but in at least fourteen schools known to the author, in various parts of the country, a similar problem exists. All are in populous urban areas, all are sadly overcrowded except one— a girl's high school in a proud Gulf city.

This school is housed in a huge, ramshackle building dating back to the days of Roosevelt—Teddy Roosevelt! Although drafty and with few modern facilities, it is unquestionably spacious. So spacious, indeed, that teachers complain they find it impossible to patrol.

As a result, weird incidents flourish in the basements and even on stairways.

Witness this, from a local police record: it seems that on the principal's complaint a 15-year-old girl was picked up by detectives for examination. A teacher had discovered her on the stairs, disheveled, her blouse torn off. She had refused to answer the teacher's questions, and it was her generally sullen attitude which had caused her to be turned over to the law. The record described her as very obese, poorly dressed and "non-cooperative." Finally she responded to persistent examination by a policewoman assigned to the local juvenile court:

I was going on an errand to the office for Miss L——. I was taking my time. Coming up the "gate" (little-used staircase connecting main building and junior high-school annex) I ran into two girls and one was smoking. I told them they'd better get back to class or they'd be in trouble. They said, what was I doing out of class? I showed them my pass. One said, did I want a cigarette? She put her arm around me and started touching me. She said, stick around and have some fun, Fatty.

I was scared. I figured they were Florabels. I tried to run. One grabbed me from behind. She tore off the blouse I was wearing, my sister's. She squeezed me and did bad things. They said they would stick cigarettes in my eyes if I didn't do bad things with them. They heard someone coming and ran. I ran but the teacher caught me.

Inquiry revealed this to be the only case of the kind on the police record in two years. As a rule, teachers and school authorities preferred to cope with such incidents as best they could without calling in police or other agencies. Perhaps they felt, with justification, that correction of the matter lay more within the province of the schools than the courts; perhaps they merely feared scandal. At first the principal refused all information to an interviewer (not this author), but after exacting a written promise not to divulge places or names, he answered interrogation as follows:

Question: Are there many such incidents in your school?

Answer: This is the seventh reported this year. (1948-49) How many go unreported, I don't know.

Question: Would coeducation help?

Answer: I'm not sure. I have reason to think so.

Question: In one city we know of, much of this trouble goes on in an all-colored school. What about the segregated schools here?

Answer: Nothing of the sort is going on in the Negro schools, so far as I know. They have their own troubles, but not this kind.

Question: To what do you attribute the trouble?

Answer: Hard to say. It sprang up during the war years, with all kinds of people coming in from all over, living under all kinds of conditions. You've got to remember, we must take care of the good kids, some teaching has to go on! We simply haven't enough manpower to cover all parts of the buildings at all times, just for the sake of a handful of bad apples.

Question: Don't they spoil the rest of the barrel?

Answer: To a certain extent. But most who get into trouble are rather curious and willing to begin with. They come from the same shack neighborhoods as the Florabels. They've heard about it. And the innocents that are pulled in—well, what can we do? They hardly ever talk. Scared to death of the Florabels! When we do catch one we punish her, maybe get rid of her.

Question: About manpower, have you tried student assistants, monitors?

Answer: Maybe that would work with boys. Here student monitors get coerced or beaten up.

The police, it turned out, were familiar enough with the "Florabels." "Call it a gang or call it a secret club, like," a newspaper reporter was told, "but one thing sure . . . the girls are bad ones! Mostly from one neighborhood. We watch the kids in the streets and keep 'em from giving much trouble, but in the school—not our job."

Whose job is it? This particular city, this pride of the South, had greatly mushroomed during the war; so had juvenile delinquency of every kind. The war's end found school population increased practically twice, school personnel hardly at all. Only a bare semblance of youth welfare or reclamation work is carried on at present writing, most of it of the volunteer "mayor's committee" type. The sole closely organized anti-delinquency effort seems to be that of Catholic groups serving chiefly the Negro and foreign-speaking elements, but even this is severely limited in scope and effect.

In a certain smoky coal-and-iron metropolis, traditionally boss-ruled, conditions in two school districts got so out of hand that a disgusted social worker for a private foundation went over the heads of her superiors—directly to the local newspapers. She offered dozens of case histories in evidence, demanded that something be done.

The first paper informed her, frankly, that the material was too raw; it prided itself on being a "family" newspaper. The second paper, as frankly, stated that publication might be taken as an attack on the Board of Education, the city administration and the powers-that-be generally—something it didn't care to risk. A third daily insisted that publicity would only make things worse, as had an exposé of the city's notorious red-light areas it had tried some months before. Said the city editor:

"This is a tough town. We've been handling delinquency pretty well! What can you expect from those drunken, no-good families . . . ?"

This same case worker privately told the author: "The

things happening in locker rooms and lavatories are unbelievable! We don't have access to school premises, so our bureau can't cope with it—no one seems able to, or is even interested!"

Doesn't a certain amount of homosexual play crop up even in the best places, she was asked.

"Not on public property, with unwholesome effects on dozens of adolescents who otherwise would never get near it! And it isn't play. It's systematic . . . A group or groups of girls who indulge simply terrorize others into doing likewise."

What was the practical answer?

"Some day society may eliminate the fundamental personality or environmental origins. Meanwhile, stronger old-fashioned control would at least protect innocent girls. The kids should never be left unsupervised except briefly; every corner in the school should be watched. But classrooms are overflowing. Doubling up of classes is common, and children are always moving about by themselves. Double the number of teachers and you still wouldn't have enough."

From all this we see a pattern emerging. Schools in crowded, badly housed or slum districts—lack of clean, modern school facilities—want of plentiful, qualified supervision and teaching—and a "bunch," a gang or "club," a "group" of girls. Acquiring recruits through seduction or force, the latter perpetuates vice from year to year, maintaining "membership" even though older ringleaders are being constantly graduated or otherwise eliminated.

So-called "gangs" among girls are not common. They number statistically about one girl gang to three hundred boy gangs! Cliques, groups, clubs and tight circles of acquaintanceship, of course, are myriad as the stars. It is only when these get out of hand, when they function in defiance of mores and custom, that they acquire the "gang" designation.

Such gang-groupings are frequent enough among boys, so much so that in a goodly number of American cities they are the rule in many parts of town rather than the exception.

Street-gangsterism and the compulsions behind it will be discussed later. Here we are concerned only with gang phenomena as a function or concomitant of schooling.

The gang which persists in a school for long periods, despite anything authorities try to do, generally is held together by powerful glue, by a strong *raison d'être*. This may be defense or offense, racial tension, rebellion against some authority or condition, superior organization for marauding or pilfering, or, as in the case of the Florabels, plain sex. Despite the high incidence of street-gangs, gangsterism of any great proportions is relatively infrequent in the schools. It seems to be more a function of idleness, of crowded streets and unpleasant homes, of sheer boredom. However, school gangsterism does exist even at quite early age levels. Every big-city teacher knows the experience of talking to some shaking child of nine or ten, robbed of a baseball glove in the school yard or adjacent streets. "I won't tell," hysterically responds the child, pressed to name his assailants. "It's the such-and-such gang! You talk, and they break your arm. Maybe kill you!"

Of course, much of the terror lies in the child's imagination. Sensitivity, immaturity, make him take threats pretty seriously.

Yet there is no denying that small-fry gangs readily evolve even well below the sixth grade.

For tykes admire and imitate their elders. Thus, when the recent death of a 15-year-old member of Brownsville's "Black Hat" gang brought its boys much publicity and police attention, even 8- and 9-year-olds wanted some of the glamour.

"They made up the most obscene password you could think of," said a teacher, referring to such a gang at P.S. 56, Sutter Avenue and Legion Street, New York. "They are only fourth and fifth graders, but extremely impressionable." She reported that they concentrated on what they called "bull-dozing." "The gang walks along, forming a solid mass to push pedestrians off the sidewalk."

Junior high schools in so-called "delinquency areas" are prone to more serious infection; sometimes even teachers are terrorized. In metropolitan high and vocational schools the tendency begins to run the other way: group activity tends to take less destructive directions—perhaps because education to the social ideal has had more time to sink in, perhaps because the worst offenders have been weeded out in the earlier grades and sent to special classes, or have dropped by the wayside and are out in the streets.

Arson, when it occurs in schools, is generally an individual matter—an expression of bitter resentment, or simply a thrill crime. But wilful destruction of school property, sneak thievery, injury to persons considered *non grata,* these are as often as not genuine gangwork. Among boys, no systematic homosexualism in the public schools is known to exist as among girls; the worst offenses are occasional mutual masturbation and maybe pretty rough treatment of a lad's private parts during a gang raid or hazing. Nor do gangs as such—in public schools, at any rate—go in for group molestation of the opposite sex. Indeed, from the best figures available, it would seem that coeducation has an inhibiting effect on adolescent crime—if not on adolescent "sin." The better record, however, may be a statistical accident. Coeducational schools are more frequently found in prosperous than in underprivileged neighborhoods.

One of the most common delinquencies of the school gang is extortion, a nickel or a soda, say, being the price of personal safety.

One case which recently made the papers (possibly because of the large amounts of money involved) had a peculiar twist or two. We quote Guy Richards, of the Hearst newspapers:

> Three years ago, investigation shows, Betty was "overly shy and sensitive." Since her mother was away from the house during the daytime, Betty was given 50 to 75 cents daily to buy lunch (at school).
>
> Almost every day on her way to school Betty was held up by two boys and two girls who took the money. Some-

times they left her 10 or 15 cents. They told her, according to a welfare report, that "they'd beat her up if she
didn't keep her mouth shut."

For a whole school year Betty lost weight. Her mother
took her to a doctor to find out what was "devouring" her.
But Betty—in that year of fear and shyness—never told.

One day Betty was taken in hand by a girl who convinced her she needed the protection of another gang.
Betty joined. Her personality changed rapidly. She entered into rivalry with another girl for leadership, the test
resolving itself into which of the two dared assault one of
the boy leaders, now in the hospital.

Betty's crime? She beat up this boy member of a rival
gang, then hammered him with a knuckle-fitted milk can
handle, then shot him through the toe with a home-made
"zip gun."

Twice she has been in court for committing mayhem on
girls. She comes from a good family. . . .

At the time of the assault, Betty was fifteen. Did her
school fail her? Yes . . . but only insofar as all society
failed her; her parents, her home, her environment, her cultural orientation, the influences shaping her personality.

How much, then, of the delinquency in and about schools
is actually the schools' fault? A good deal of it, is the answer—yet only in a secondary sense. The school is not an
independent entity; it is an expression of the community
which gives it funds and direction. It can only do what it is
equipped and authorized to do.

Certainly if all classes were small enough, if teachers were
plentiful enough, if quality of personnel were improved by
paying higher salaries, if there were more and better facilities, delinquency would be set back. Certainly if there were
more guidance workers, psychologists and psychiatrists attached to school systems, more could be done to correct delinquent tendencies arising out of the personality of the child
or the deficiencies of his environment. But all this depends
on the desire of the citizenry. They get more than they pay
for, as it is.

Admittedly, the school is not wholly blameless. More could be done, doubtless, in the way of reshaping curriculums and adjusting organization for handling pre-delinquents, and for protecting the general student body from actual delinquents. (The term *pre-delinquent* applies to children considered potentially delinquent, or predisposed to delinquency.)

Where an exceptionally forceful and interested school executive takes over, sometimes miracles occur. We might mention, for example, a notorious junior high school located on New York's lower east side, formerly considered one of the worst "delinquency" spots in the country. Boys were completely unmanageable. Every type of crime and vicious mischief was common. Teachers were so involved in discipline problems that little time remained for anything else. Then the school was turned over to a young assistant principal who by fearless, conscientious effort, and intelligent understanding, instilled group pride and a modicum of good behavior into his boys. Some of his means were radical. He found outlets for the animal spirits of his charges, instead of trying to bottle them up. He encouraged responsibility, appointing some of the worst offenders to class and group leadership (this trick often works). He held the facilities of the school open after school hours, to keep the boys off the streets. He reached into their homes through personal contact.

In the short space of a year this school, while not yet exactly a model, had taken its place among the best to be found in similar neighborhoods!

One impotant factor contributing to delinquency, all authorities agree, is daily absence from home of both parents. Children of working mothers—called "latchkey kids" among teachers—constitute a problem of major proportions in communities large and small throughout the nation. Supervised playgrounds provide a partial answer in many cities; but these are far too few. The school is expected to contribute, in some places, by extra-curricular activity, by "clubs" for dancing, drama, picknicking and the like. All too often, teachers are unpaid for this overtime drain on their physical and nervous energy. Paid teachers exclusively assigned to such club work, as in four underprivileged New York City school districts, accomplished better results; local "latchkey" kids have a place to go where they may play constructively, and so perhaps keep out of trouble.

On the whole, it may be stated teachers individually are doing as much as can be expected of them, and a lot more, with respect to combating delinquency. As much cannot be said for the school systems which they serve, nor for the communities of which the school is an instrument and expression.

4

Vice in Private Schools

So FAR WE HAVE TOUCHED ON THE RELATIONSHIP ONLY of the public schools to juvenile delinquency. What of non-public schools? Have they any special culpability for the climbing juvenile crime rate?

America, particularly in the New England and Middle Atlantic areas, boasts an educational coat of many colors. It sports a patchwork of parochial, private and institutional schools of every style and size. Take your pick! Here are establishments for poor and rich. Boarding schools range from "preparatory" institutes for the scions of our best people to "homes" for backward or wayward children. There are military and "finishing" schools. Is your son deaf, crippled or simply unwanted? You send him to a special *alma mater*, if you have the price—sometimes even if you haven't. Are you particular about what your daughter is allowed to learn or not learn? You may choose from among great parochial systems maintained by religious denominations, lesser ones supported by political sects, or from schools conducted by fringe groups of all kinds, by foundations or individuals—some non-profit, others out for every dollar they can get.

Inevitably, delinquency plagues these schools just as it does public ones.

Yet it must be conceded that the "private" record is better. At least on the surface.

Why not? The problems of badly crowded classes—insufficient staffs—less frequently exist.

Control and authority are absolute, often extending over even the non-classroom hours.

In the case of parochial schools, offenders are quickly passed on to denominational "welfare" and "correction"

40

facilities, or simply thrown back into the laps of the public schools—which take on all comers.

But while they may reach the surface less frequently in and around the non-public school, this is not to say that delinquency and pre-delinquency, when they appear, are better handled. On the contrary. The public school, by its very nature, gives kids more chance to blow off steam, to adjust themselves naturally for better or worse, to get rid of personality quirks by simple attrition. In this respect, most private institutions are better at repressing and suppressing than at curing. If predisposing factors of delinquency are present in him at all, many a product of these schools, once escaped from their confines, explodes.

There is no reason to believe that schools under religious or private auspices are doing any better than the public schools. But the point remains that in Catholic as in other parochial and private schools, education has failed to meet the challenge of delinquency. There are numerous Catholic agencies devoted to the "bad" boy or girl; despite religious scruples which stand in way of adopting certain psychiatric techniques—or perhaps because of these very scruples— some progress is being made each year. But this progress does not keep pace with delinquency's present spread. The same is true of Protestant and Jewish groups maintaining settlement houses in crowded areas, as well as reform homes, camps, correction farms and the like. What the anti-delinquency fight requires is not less participation by organized religion, but more.

As for genteel, non-parochial institutions, everyone remembers the wave of delinquency which spread among even the most respectable private schools during the war. Such cases as this one became almost standard reading:

> Four 16-year-old students at a famous New Jersey academy are being held in Warren County Jail at Belvidere, today, three charged with arson and all four with larceny of automobiles. The boys burned a barn and attempted to burn an adjoining farmhouse. They were apprehended by state troopers.

This academy ranks among the most respected institutions of its kind, generally having managed to avoid even the sex and drinking excesses which commonly trouble "prep" schools. Another typical case involving private school adolescents—so typical that almost its very twin appeared in newspapers every day all over the land—involved three girls reported missing from a well-known and expensive New England girls' school.

A detective located the first girl soliciting in the streets. He watched her tease a prospect—a merchant seaman—into going with her to the fifth-floor room of a hotel. "The sailor offered her five dollars," testified the detective. "She took the money and removed her clothes. I then entered the room and made the arrest."

The second girl, a 15-year-old, also was picked up by a detective. He offered her five dollars. She accepted. He arrested her.

The third girl was picked up by police while soliciting in a bus terminal.

Three kids from one of our most ladylike finishing schools!

Now, such offenses were the order of the day during the war years and immediately afterward. So much so that our good citizenry hardly took notice of them—except to smack lips over the gory or titillating details. Professional viewers-with-alarm, civic groups and police, even J. Edgar Hoover himself, might be much disturbed, but the reaction of the man in the street was more or less: "So many homes unsettled. Soldiers and sailors out for a good time. Easy war plant money. You have to expect wraps off . . . Morals are always bad in wartime!" Perhaps so. But the war is over. Why does delinquency persist, even in "good" schools? Why is delinquency, despite temporary setbacks and fluctuations, on the increase everywhere? Do the conditions of the war years remain with us?

Not all of them, of course. But bad and insufficient housing, one of delinquency's greatest allies, continues on every hand. The easy money is beginning to be replaced by lack of money—more than 4,000,000 unemployed at this writing, and some 6,000,000 not working a full-time week. Jobs for teen-agers, part time or otherwise, are growing scarce as the ham in drugstore sandwiches. Impoverishment, and attendant idleness, are far greater hand-maidens of crime than prosperity ever was.

Further, there are certain moral hangovers from the war. Or, viewed another way, the moral climate which makes both war and delinquency possible is still with us. Millions of men, though out of uniform, preserve attitudes toward sex and violence acquired in the armed services. Millions of girls retain the "easy come, easy go" views on virtue believed appropriate during the war years. Most of these have grown beyond the age limits considered "juvenile," but their younger sisters and brothers ape their outlooks, as no doubt their children will.

With patriotism out as motivation and excuse, the modern schoolgirl may ask and receive a higher price for her sex— inflation being what it is. In better-class private schools, where money is no object, she may trade for social triumphs, dates with football idols, simple excitement, or even a passing mark.

But sex is far from the only excess troubling juvenile officers. Nine murders (several linked with homosexualism), one hundred and nineteen injuries requiring hospitalization, twelve off-campus larceny cases, three arson offenses, forty-three vandalism raids above the mischief class, three rapes, fourteen statutory rapes, one hundred and forty-nine "seductions" worthy of court interest, various extortion-type situations, and eighteen assorted crimes such as the carrying of blackjacks—these were recorded last year alone on police and court records of New England and New York State, on the part of students attending private schools.

Considering the large numbers of students at such places, some would not regard these figures as too disturbing. Maybe they are right. The really disturbing thing is the extent to which student bodies as a general practice are imitating the let-down in standards all around them. Lying, cheating, fornicating, unsportsmanlike conduct, never giving the other fellow an even break, all the things frowned on by decent people, these would seem to be tolerated to a greater extent than during the pre-war years. We do not mean to say that the youth of America is rotten. Far from it! It is a more vigorous youth than ever before, healthier physically and mentally, more intelligent in attitude and action. But it includes a greater segment than ever before of boys and girls lacking the stringent moral precepts by which a society retains its honor and health.

How can kids take "fair play" seriously, for example, when they note so many examples of doubtful practices in business—giving the least for the most, making extravagant claims for shoddy goods? How can they cultivate independent thought when they note penalties for independence on every hand? Better to move with the mob. Better to accept the hypocrisies of modern life, whereby millions decry conditions publicly which privately they foster.

On the whole, then, the crime problem of private schools approximates that of public schools. It varies in degree, perhaps, but very little in kind. Institutions serving underprivileged students drawn from a broad population base run into the usual patterns of gangsterism, theft, marauding. Where students are more selective, as a result of wealth, intelligence, educational background or other entrance requirements, offenses may be more imaginative, and tend toward sex, "thrill" crimes, wild escapades and the like.

Yet there is one particularly noxious area of delinquency which is far more the province of private than of public schools. As previously remarked, where millions of students come into daily and somewhat intimate contact with thousands of teachers, some degree of sexual abuse is bound to appear. In private schools, however, as contrasted with public ones, teacher-student carnality approaches the dimensions of an appalling problem. Why is this so? Chiefly because of greater opportunity for the indulgence of mature appetites—and the awakening of immature ones.

Private schools, including penal ones, are subject to the same general controls as public educational institutions. But such schools are many and diverse. They function in all sorts of dark corners as well as out in the light of day, so that for one reason or another they escape inspection, or get around it. Sometimes they are less severe than is wise in judging qualifications of personnel. In some types of institutions, the pupils are cut off from the protection of parents, may not even have parents. They can be got at during odd hours, and in privacy. Facilities, such as beds, are available. Further, while most states have licensing requirements for both private schools and private school teachers, these vary greatly, in many cases are not effective. The result is an annual crop of such incidents as these, all from recent records:

(1) At a New York orphan asylum, two employes were charged with immoral practices on inmates of both sexes. One, 58, had been engineer at the home for twenty-six years. The other was a staff teacher. During Grand Jury investigation twenty-seven boys and girls, 8 to 16, appeared as witnesses. Conducted by a Protestant church group, the asylum at the time housed a total of fifty-one children.

(2) At an institution for rehabilitation of the deaf, conducted under state auspices, three girls were found by a visiting doctor to be pregnant. Two were 13, the third 14. All three, under questioning, cited the father to be the assistant superintendent.

(3) Four instructors, three male and one female, at a swank Connecticut school, were arrested on complaint of the landlady of a wealthy student, aged 13. When this boy's apartment was raided, authorities found two instructors in bed with two boy students and a girl, the other pair of instructors in bed with two girl students. One 14-year-old student was so drunk she had to be carried to the patrol wagon.

In addition, there occurs each year a certain number of cases involving recreational and Sunday school pupils, rather than those attending "schools" in a more formal sense:

(1) A West Virginia minister slays a choir girl with a hammer. She had threatened to disclose immoral practices between the minister and various girls attending Sunday School.

(2) A minister of White Plains is held on charges of carnally abusing two boys, brothers and members of his parish. He admits the crimes, says he is a "damned fool."

(3) A one-time champion tennis player is jailed for a second time on charges of immoral acts conducted in broad daylight in public places with students at his "tennis school."

(4) At a large military institute, three instructors are fired and three students expelled. They were in the habit of bringing in prostitutes and sharing them in a dormitory. One of the instructors was 70.

But we are concerned here with juvenile, not adult, crime.

The question may well be asked: how are the juveniles involved in these cases to be construed "delinquent"? Are they not more sinned against than sinning? The answer is yes, and as much may be said for most delinquents, whether sexual offenders or not. But the significant thing is the effect of these school abuses, the influences contributing to the birth and spread of delinquency. What we glimpse is a Fagin-like source, and a kind of transmission belt; among the backwashes of education, children are being taught—or forced—to tolerate sex conduct considered evil. If the inoculation takes, the students themselves then spread the virus upon graduation or release. They embrace "sin" and teach it, even as their betters did. Once infected, each one may become a carrier, a Typhoid Mary of depravity.

The foregoing discussion may bring to the reader's mind that notorious English school, Horsley Hall, widely discussed in American newspapers before it was finally shuttered by authorities.

At this remarkable institution, teen-aged students were encouraged to do "whatever comes to them naturally."

"My boys and girls go into each other's bedrooms," said Robert Copping, headmaster, "but I see nothing wrong with that." They also smoked if it suited them, and used four-letter words. Official tolerance tended to cut down smoking and swearing, claimed Copping. His pupils rose and retired when they pleased, studied only when in the mood.

Unfortunately, the bearded, 29-year-old headmaster admitted in court to having spent a week end in London with a student of sixteen.

And the court accused Charles Reynolds, partner of Copping, of utilizing his living room as a bedroom for two girl students. The crown prosecutor also claimed that in Reynolds' presence, one boy dared another to seduce a certain girl pupil. According to the prosecutor, Reynolds said: "I bet you a pound to a penny you can't!"

The incident, however, which first attracted official notice was none of these. It seems that Copping invited one Eric A. Wildman, who supplies schools with canes for punishing malefactors, to visit Horsley Hall. Copping then arranged for his pupils to beat up Mr. Wildman with his own canes—a bit of poetic justice which promptly brought court investigation, and closing.

Well, the Copping idea of liberal arts may be a bit broad for general application. But milder variations of it are plentifully encountered in this and other lands. In "self-expression" and "progressive" schools of high and low degree, adolescents are encouraged to live by the rule of conscience rather than that of authority.

Is that bad? To be sure, the trust is not always repaid. Especially where it is convenient for the sexes to mingle. A nice prep-school boy obtaining mutual sex experience with a nice finishing-school girl may not be a crime in the eyes of nature; but it remains delinquency by generally accepted codes. These persist in holding intercourse a crime unless indulged in at certain ages, and after certain ceremonies.

Yet an investigation by no less august a body than the New York Academy of Medicine, conducted among college students, led it to this estimate: a majority of such males experience the sex act by the age of sixteen. The Kinsey report yields somewhat parallel indications for non-college males below twenty-one. At any rate, it would seem that the precocious sex indulgences of boys and girls of school age are so common as to hardly be regarded as more than technical delinquency.

Even early prostitution, unless involuntary, is not inevitably to be considered crime per se, for it rarely hurts or deprives. Rape and robbery, on the other hand, where force and injury rule, are patently criminal in our society. By extension, schools tolerating the freedoms or even excesses with which youth matures are not to be classed therefore as delinquency breeding grounds. Not so with institutions and schools which give courses in forced submission, equivalent to rape. To what extent foulness can flourish is illustrated in the Balles case commented on at length in the press a couple of years back.

Late one winter's Saturday a man of 33 sat in a parked car near Norristown, Pa. With him, supine and yielding, was a girl. A young girl. Eleven years old.

A passing police car stopped to investigate. The cops did not relish what they saw. They ordered the passionate parker to start up his motor and follow their car to a police station for questioning. The man and child drove after the police car for a short distance, then suddenly swung off at an intersection and fled.

Later the two were discovered hiding in the home of a neighborhood friend. The girl was taken to Abington Hospital. The man, having admitted molesting her, was locked up in Montgomery County Jail. Subsequent grand jury and court proceedings brought out a tale as harrowing as any in the history of private schools.

The man? George W. Balles, headmaster and owner of the Warminster Academy, later characterized by the court as a "School for Immorality." The academy operated in a 23-room converted farmhouse at Three Tuns, not far from Norristown. The student body consisted of twenty-eight boys and girls of middle-class families in Pennsylvania, New Jersey and New York, ages ranging from 7 to 14 years.

Questioning of the children and the headmaster brought facts to light that were so shocking as to turn the stomachs of the examiners.

Almost no depth of sex degradation, it seemed, had not been plumbed by Balles in the company of his students, both boys and girls. These children were taught to submit voluntarily to every bestiality, or were forced into it. Up to the time of the school's closing, the kind of creatures being manufactured at Warminster can only be imagined.

Nor was that the worst of it. Perhaps the most unnatural part in the proceedings was that attributed to the man's wife, Laura, a woman of 35. She was accused of participating in the orgies and forcing children to submit to her husband.

The court charged George W. Balles with statutory rape, assault and battery, contributing to the delinquency of minors, corrupting public morals. Mrs. Balles was charged with contributing to the delinquency of minors, corrupting public morals and compounding a felony.

Six months later, on appeal, Judge Harold C. Knight denied a new trial to Balles, sustaining conviction on charges of rape, morals and contributing to delinquency. He faced a sentence of up to forty-eight years. To Mrs. Balles, however, who could have been sentenced to more than twenty-two years, the judge granted a new trial. Referring to the tale of a 14-year-old who had testified against her, he found it "too unnatural to warrant belief!"

George W. Balles represented himself as a minister. He and his wife had a child five years old. To all appearances, they and their school were perfectly respectable. So once again we see that the conduct of private schools in this country should never get too "private." No state or local authority can afford to relax its vigilance. Inspection should reach at regular intervals into the premises and practices of every school, no matter how large or small, no matter how well-reputed, and no matter how unobtrusively located.

5

Thou Shalt Not Kill

FEW TRAGEDIES HOLD MORE SORROW THAN THE DEATH of one child at the hands of another. The slayer is hardly less a victim than the slain, hardly less to be pitied.

We wonder what torture of mind, what bitter twist of circumstance, could have driven a child to kill. We doubt whether the offender realizes the enormity of his crime. We are not sure he so much as knows right from wrong, especially under the passionate stresses prevailing at the time of the assault. The courts reflect our attitude. Usually they hold the adolescent not sufficiently responsible to incur the punishments meted out to adult killers.

Yet numerous enough instances are recorded of children under 16 being made to suffer the fullest penalties, including death.

A recent New Jersey case serves as an example:

So swept by emotion it is doubtful he heard the court's words, 15-year-old Fred S—— was sentenced to between 25 and 30 years in New Jersey State Prison by Hudson County Judge Stanton. The prosecuting attorney had called on Judge Stanton for a "severe sentence" on the grounds of "vicious, premeditated murder." The boy's attorney was in the midst of an eloquent plea for mercy when his youthful client sobbed and his knees buckled. Fred said he murdered his playmate, 11-year-old Jackie, to "prove I am no sissy." He said he had been compelled by his parents to perform household tasks he considered fit only for women.

On the average, children up to 16 commit murder and malicious manslaughter 97 percent less often than do older persons—children and adolescents aged 21 or younger, 70 percent less often. But the favorable ratio does not derive from any lesser inclination to kill.

The fact is that youngsters feel the killing impulse—and obey it—more often than do adults!

It takes less powerful stimuli to arouse them to violent responses. They give less thought to consequences. Social penalties are not so deeply perceived, mores not as deeply implanted. Notorious are the cruelties, as well as the kindnesses, of children. Indeed, the adult murderer is often thought of as a "child who never grew up"—a person who failed to mature sufficiently to control the asocial impulses accepted as more or less commonplace among pre-adolescents.

The big difference is that with children the will, strength, and weapons to carry out the job are not often present. Hence the impulse to kill, when it does triumph over inhibitory mechanisms within the child and prohibitory ones imposed from without, usually fades or fails before the purpose is accomplished. In rage, the child swings. He misses. His club is taken away from him. His quick blow falls short of the damage intended, and once it is delivered, resentment may quickly fade or distractions occur. In any case, the reflex tends to spend itself with the single blow or a few blows, fully murderous in intent though weak in result.

Just the same, enough successful Cains distinguish the younger generation each year to justify a third major classification of delinquency. Major not because of the extent or frequency of juvenile killings, but because they are crimes of direct consequence, capital crimes. Conveniently, this class may be subdivided into a number of groups, with examples given of each.

SECONDARY KILLINGS

This group includes crimes in which killing is not the primary intent, but results as a byproduct of meanness, viciousness, carelessness or other characteristic evidencing itself in the course of the child's play or social life. Maliciousness, if present, only in a secondary sense results in the killing, which therefore cannot be classed as malicious manslaughter. It more resembles the manslaughter incurred when an adult mean or careless enough to drive recklessly runs over another. A 10-year-old boy in a small Arkansas town provides a distressing and definitive case:

One fine spring day, Robert was playing hide-and-go-seek with three neighbor children—Joyce, aged 9; Shirley, aged 6; and James, aged 2. The three decided it would be fun to hide in an old-fashioned wooden icebox, abandoned by our hero's mother in favor of more modern equipment.

Apprised by muffled giggling of the whereabouts of the children, Robert could not resist the chance to play a trick. He shut the icebox door on them. Thereupon the three became the object of a long and frantic search. Ultimately they were found, quite dead.

The 10-year-old, questioned by state police, readily confessed his part in the misdeed. After locking in the others, he explained, he had been unable to get the icebox door open. "My mother called me then, to go to the store. *Then I forgot!*" (Italics ours.)

Police and courts faced the dilemma of all of us. Said H. R. Peterson, police lieutenant in charge of the investigation: "He's too young to do anything with even if it had been deliberate—and I don't believe it was."

RAGE KILLINGS

These result from simple anger or loss of temper, closely resembling similar crimes among adults. They differ from slayings inspired by jealousy and some other emotions in that they may have sparse roots or none at all in preceding grievances against the slain. Nor are they akin to killing out of fear, which is almost killing in self-defense. They do parallel other emotional crimes, however, in that the trigger is usually some frustration. That the frustrating factor need not be very strong we can gather from such murders as this, reported in Lancaster, Pa.:

The father and mother saw no reason not to go on a jaunt for a few hours. After all, 14-year-old Millicent had been working for the family occasionally, and seemed quite capable of taking care of their son Ronald, aged 6. Millicent was instructed to do the family wash while the couple was out.

The girl started the washing-machine. Ronald wanted to play. He pulled the plug of the machine from the electric socket. The girl pushed the plug into place; Ronald pulled it out again. This went on for some time. Then Millicent lost her temper. She grabbed a piece of wood "two inches thick and sixteen inches long" and beat Ronald about the head.

Five hours later he died in a hospital.

THRILL KILLINGS

Like other types of crime, murder may be indulged in by both child and adult solely for the sake of exhilaration. To wish to kill another human being simply for the sensation of killing is universally regarded as pathological, requiring, at very least, heroic treatment by an alienist. The wish to kill birds, beasts or fishes for the same reason, however, in many circles is accepted as normal. Killing, whether of man or lesser creature, seems to offer an expression of power tempting to many. In addition, there are killings which occur as a secondary result of other thrill-seeking behavior, *thrill* being here used to denote sensual or emotional exaltation.

Witness this deed of derring-do:

While his father, a produce merchant, happened to be in Cuba on a trip, a 14-year-old boy ran across a .32 caliber revolver somewhere about his home. Probably Dad's, he figured; and if the head of the house could play with such things, why not the son? And why not call in Phillip, a good friend, to share the "thrill" of handling an honest-to-goodness gun?

Phillip, 12 years old, enthusiastically joined the fun. But just handling and playing with the weapon wasn't enough. Kids don't get hold of a revolver every day! What further sensations could the boys aspire to, with such a thrill-productive treasure in their possession? Remembering a movie they had seen, they decided to play "Russian roulette."

So they placed one cartridge in the gun's chamber—just one little cartridge. The host spun the chamber first. He pointed it at the floor and pulled the trigger. A click. Nothing happened. Then Phillip, not to be outdone in bravado, took the weapon.

He spun the chamber, pointed the barrel at his head . . . and he too pulled the trigger.

He died in Jewish Hospital, Brooklyn.

Murder, definitely, albeit self-murder. But who was the murderer? Phillip himself? His friend who found the gun? His friend's father who left it where it could be found? Society—school—parents—for failing to instill balance and responsibility in the boys, or at least a proper fear of death?

Take your choice of culprits. But this might be the place to point out that not all "latchkey" children have working mothers or live in impoverished homes. Neglected children are to be found in prosperous surroundings as well.

All too often, little Tommy's mother is so busy with bridge and shopping that she pays little attention to him; besides, she can afford a servant or two. Tommy has a backyard to play in, and "nice" friends, and does not usually come into contaminating contact with the crass street delinquency of the slums. Yet in the absence of parental interest and guidance, he too can burst the dams of propriety. When he does, he may become more dangerous to himself and society than his bad-neighborhood counterpart.

The delinquency problem is one not only of quantity, but of quality. There are intensities of delinquency, as well as grades and types. Tommy, healthier and with more advantages than many boys to begin with, when he does take up crime is inclined to go to the head of the class. Thus, the Variety Clubs of America, which have been in the thick of the delinquency fight for many years, report that more than 60 per cent of the "really dangerous" delinquents come from homes of "middle" or "upper" class. These are the delinquents whose crimes consist of murder, armed robbery,

larceny—rather than simple assault, truancy or swiping
from the five-and-ten.

"Delinquency," reported J. Edgar Hoover in 1947, "is
increased by parents, who are too busy with their own pleasures to give sufficient time, companionship and interest to
their children." And such delinquency, among juveniles
of otherwise good background, takes the form of a "thrill"
crime far more often than it does among the underprivileged. A good many of the latter's sins result from needs
for something concrete—money, clothes, shelter, food, play
space. Your more fortunate child, who has these concrete
things, commits misdeeds based on wants for spiritual or
emotional satisfactions; hence the relatively high incidence
of thrill crimes—malicious mischief grown out of its
breeches, and indulged in, most often, as a result of emotional lack or stultification:

A police officer found the nude body of a 10-year-old boy
hidden in a culvert on a country road. He had been horribly slashed, mangled beyond hope of recognition. There
was nothing by which to identify him, since his clothing
could not be found.

Months of tenacious police work traced the murderers—
two high-school students who had sought to commit a "perfect crime." Reading that the police had confessed themselves unable to identify their victim's body, the students
had brazenly visited the morgue to name him; and they
had helped the police in other ways just to see if their crime
was really beyond solution.

No other motive existed. Both boys had money and all
the comforts of life. Neither had any quarrel with the murdered child.

A thrill crime. . . .

When the thrill crime aspires to murder, the question of
how to handle the culprit becomes an especially delicate
one. Ideally, shall he be treated like other delinquents—
retrained for a period, and if he responds, told to go and
sin no more? Logically, his transgression springs, like lesser

delinquencies, from a personality disturbance. Logically again, should the disturbance be removed and the offender reconditioned to proper behavior, he becomes fit as a fiddle for the normal life. But the logic goes further. Suppose the cure is faulty? The best of men make mistakes—and the best of child experts. The commendable hopefulness of professionals sometimes induces even them to assume that disappearance of symptoms means cure of basic cause, when actually it may signify no more than palliation. Or suppose the cure is apparently successful, but new environmental circumstances in the "cured" offender's later life bring back the same or another personality disturbance? Will the boy again murder?

Parallel questions were raised in the recent case of a barber committed to a Long Island mental hospital under a diagnosis of *dementia praecox*. More than a year afterward, he was pronounced cured and his release sought by the hospital. His family, particularly his wife, strenuously objected. She feared him. She refused to accept him in her household. The hospital, crowded and put to what it considered unfair expense to retain a number of similarly "cured" patients, decided to make a test case out of the barber and went to court. The judges held in the hospital's favor. How could they do otherwise? Two noted psychiatrists swore that the barber was completely cured, completely normal. One testified that the man was thoroughly fit to go back to his trade!

Perhaps so. The point is that even eminent experts can be mistaken. Who would want to sit in a chair with this particular barber wielding the razor?

Similarly, releasing a thrill murderer may be justified by the evidence—but is all the evidence in, and is it always infallible? Certain well-intentioned probationary and psychiatric experts are stricken by the injustice of holding a boy who apparently no longer has anything wrong with him. They claim that in any case close surveillance and control of environment can avoid the consequences of error. But are thorough controls feasible except in some form of custody? A slip might prove costly.

This is no matter of stealing, truancy or the like—the recurrence of which does not drastically curtail life. Nor is it a matter of murder committed for reasons anti-social, but in a sense rational: to get away from a cop, to rob, to eliminate competition in love. The thrill killing, except to the thrill killer, represents the height of irrationality. And irrationality, experts notwithstanding, in the present state of human knowledge remains unpredictable. Further, it would seem that at least something may be said for the old-fashioned idea of imprisonment for its deterrent example to others. In Joliet, Ill., for example, lives a plump, freckled-faced little girl, thirteen years old, by the name of Susie:

Susie had been entranced by stories in the newspapers about Harold, 14, the confessed thrill killer of a playmate. Avidly following the reports, Susie read that the judge in Harold's case finally ruled the boy incapable of telling the difference between right and wrong. He ordered Harold released. . . .

Susie promptly went out and drowned her own playmate, 7-year-old James C——, in a drainage ditch.

"I don't know why I did it," she stated to officers. "He hadn't done anything. I just had an urge to push him in the water."

Before confessing the murder, she helped search for the victim's body, and was good enough to take up a collection for a floral wreath at the funeral.

SEX KILLINGS

Included in this group is that most obnoxious of crimes, the murder for purposes of direct erotic satisfaction:

An unpleasant smell lingered about the old well. As though a skunk had been paying visits, or something rotten had been flung into its depths. The family owning the property on which the well stood were planning to sell. To better their chances, they sent for a man to investigate the odor. He climbed down the shaft, returned in a few minutes, pale and shaking.

"There's a body down there. Maybe two. I ain't sure," he said.

Police, investigating, took the decayed bodies of two young girls from the well shaft. Finally they arrested a flabby youth, owner of a shiny new automobile.

It had been his pleasure, the police testified during the trial, to run down pretty girls with his autombile. He would then rape the newly slaughtered or still-kicking bodies, and fling them into any handy pit.

Such glaring perversion almost never is found among youngsters. It is as if they have not yet had time to develop the deep, pent repressions or sexual twists which in aberrational adults can find release in such crimes. Emotional disease in a child has not yet progressed to the point where orgasm may be assisted through the sight of blood, the act of giving death, the infliction of pain.

Adolescent sadism has no demonstrated roots in sex, despite occasional protestations to the contrary by certain psychoanalysts.

No . . . the identifying circumstance of most murders here called *sex killings* is merely that they took place *during* pursuit of sexual satisfaction, or as a result of it—but in response to drives other than sexual ones. Except for the fortuitous factor of sex, they might very well be grouped otherwise—under *rage killings, secondary killings, thrill killings* and other categories yet to be given. Here is a crime, for example, where the sex element is rudimentary; fear or accident being the immediate cause of death. It involves one Justin, the youngest person ever to be indicted on a first-degree murder charge in his community of nearly a million population:

All Justin sought was information. Like Eve, he bit of the apple, trusting that the knowledge thus achieved would eventually lead him to the sexual satisfactions every male pursues. It began when his parents decided to go out with a neighboring couple, leaving Justin as baby-sitter with the neighbors' 3-year-old Celia. Justin, aged 14, was known as a responsible boy. His elders entrusted him with the task of putting Celia to bed.

This was too good a chance to miss. Giving Celia her bath, Justin succumbed to curiosity concerning anatomical details about which his parents or school should have more fully informed him. To fill the gaps in his knowledge, he poked and probed at little Celia, examining her in great detail.

What followed remains obscure. The younger child vigorously objected, and perhaps cried out in a way that filled Justin with fear of discovery. Perhaps she threatened to tell her parents that she was being maltreated. But in any event, the ensuing scramble proved too much for tiny Celia in the water-filled bathtub. When her parents arrived home from the movies they found Celia dead. Drowned.

If Justin drowned Celia out of fear that she would talk, he was following a pattern by no means unique. Fear— whether of discovery or exposure—accounts for a good many of the "sex murders" thought to represent aberration or perversion on the part of the juvenile perpetrator.

Other emotions also are guilty of some of these sex crimes, particularly rage—at being rejected, at being foiled. Such murders recur in the history of every generation. Virtually standard are episodes of the kind involving, respectively, James who killed out of terror, and Percy who killed in anger. Both crimes took place in rural areas:

James, 13, had been sent by comfortable parents to vacation at a summer camp in Vermont. Wandering away from its confines one day, he ran across apple-cheeked Betty—strolling down a path near her home. He called greetings. Betty, aged 10, was a friendly sort, and curious about the boys at the camp. She was glad to join him for a bit of conversation, maybe a bit of play.

The play got rough. James sneaked a look around. No one watching but the birds. Anyway, this country bumpkin wouldn't mind. He threw her to the ground and assaulted her.

It turned out that Betty did mind. She shrieked. When

he had satiated himself and released her she darted off, yelling for her parents. James, in mortal fear, ran after her, caught her, shut her mouth forever—by strangling her.

*   *   *

Percy, a country boy, had been watching the dogs and horses, not to mention his elders. At 9, he did not know why he should not investigate certain phenomena for himself. Nobody had bothered to explain anything about it to him, either at home or at school, where he attended third grade.

So Percy propositioned his neighbor, the 3-year-old child of a soldier absent on duty. The infant didn't understand. When Percy tried to force his attentions on her, she presumed he wanted to fight and gave back almost as good as she got. The resistance enraged Percy. He beat her on the head with rocks until, suddenly, she stopped moving.

"I don't know why I did it," Percy later told investigators. He meant that he had wanted only to love her, not kill her.

These types of sex murder are not limited to young children; and, as a matter of fact, occur with somewhat greater frequency among adolescents between the ages of 15 and 21. It is almost always the boy, driven into an emotional corner after he has acted in response to his powerful sex drives, who commits the killing. The following history is a compilation from court, police and newspaper reports:

Rosemary, blithe and blue-eyed, could claim to be one of the prettiest and most popular girls in her large northwestern town. A sweet and lovable girl, too, active in church work and Episcopal parish affairs.

One Saturday, while helping to clean a recreation hall where a church dance was to be held, she opened the door of an unused closet. A bird, which had somehow got itself trapped in the closet, flew out and escaped through an open window. "You all had better watch out," joked Rosemary to friends present. "That means death!"

A few evenings later, she went out on a date with two girls and three boys from a nearby college. Rosemary left them early, to attend a youth meeting at the Episcopal church. But the crowd had gone off on a picnic and Rosemary found herself alone. Almost alone, that is.

We can imagine her hearing a footstep. She turns uneasily. Two attacks on women had been reported in that vicinity some weeks previously.

Before she can make out the intruder, she feels a stunning blow on the top of her head. Her thick hair saves her. She staggers, but fights desperately as she feels strong arms tearing at her dress. She claws with her nails, bites, screams for help. Her attacker, in alarm, strikes again. Still she fights and screams, manages to twist away. Now it is the assailant's turn to feel terror. If only he could shut her mouth! With all his strength, he plants a third blow on Rosemary's torn scalp; at the same time he twists a gunny sack about her neck . . . tighter . . . tighter. Rosemary is dead.

Stunned by his own deed, the killer stumbles out of the church into the night. . . .

The crime comes to light the next morning, but police find themselves stymied. The only thing they have to go on is the fact of a terrific struggle; furniture in the church room is upset and broken, shreds of skin and flesh cling to the dead Rosemary's finger nails. They broadcast an alarm for a person whose face is scratched. Meanwhile, at the local high school, good-looking Charles, the same age as Rosemary, appears in class with a countenance that looks as if cats had been fighting on it. A friend, who had been unable to keep a date with him at the church the night before—the night of the murder—cries, "What happened?" "Oak poisoning," explains Charles. This does not satisfy one of the girls in class, who happened to have heard the police broadcast. She gets word to an officer. Charles is picked up at school.

Under questioning, the boy admits hazy recollections,

vague yet horrible memories as if out of a dream. The whole town is profoundly shocked. Charles is more than handsome: he is a star athlete, a prize student, a choir-singing acolyte in the very church which served as the scene of the crime. "Everything we know about him is good," reports the church rector. "I never saw him lose his temper or self-control about anything," states his football coach.

But under the pressure of the police, Charles leads them to a gunny sack and a broken pop bottle. He shows them his stained clothing. . .

Sometimes the emotional atmosphere may not become supercharged until well after the incident which identifies the crimes as belonging to the sex killings group. Nor need the object of the sexual drive be the object of the emotional one—the fear, anger or jealousy culminating in murder:

As the long Milwaukee winter began, young Seymour found his attentions to pretty Shirley, then 17 or 18, growing rather ardent. The girl did not discourage him. On the contrary, she welcomed the companionship of Seymour, a handsome lad and an honor student at school. Affection quickly developed into intimacy. Before spring had come, Shirley learned she was pregnant.

That scared both kids. They were too young to get parental consent to marriage without revealing their misstep, which Shirley, particularly, was ashamed to do. Keeping their heads, they decided that the best thing would be to elope. But where could they go? How would they live? And would they, so young, find someone willing to marry them? Elopement would require thought and planning. Shirley took into confidence her 16-year-old sister, Frances.

The kid sister did not react exactly as expected. Not that she wasn't sympathetic, but the secret gave her intoxicating power over Shirley and Shirley's lover. Perhaps she was jealous of his passion for the older girl, or loved him herself. At any rate, she teased Shirley a bit, and Seymour unmercifully. She took to constantly threatening him with exposure. And from later testimony it would appear that she did finally tattle to someone—parents or friends.

Then one day Frances disappeared. A month later, by purest chance, dredgers hauled up her body out of the Milwaukee River. She had been shot twice in the head. Attached to her leg, for a sinker, was a 38-pound concrete block.

Two days before, Shirley and Seymour had also disappeared. Police located them in Minneapolis, where they had succeeded in getting married and were looking for jobs. In testimony later stricken from the court record, Shirley was quoted by police as saying that all through the honeymoon she had been thinking of her sister and at night would cry herself to sleep; she had had "A hunch ever since Frances disappeared that Seymour had a part in it." But under further questioning by the police, and later in court, she attempted to cover up for him.

Her loyalty did not help Seymour. In an hour and twenty minutes a Milwaukee jury found him guilty. There is no capital punishment in Wisconsin; he was sentenced to life imprisonment.

Shirley snubbed her mother and others who accepted Seymour's guilt. With her baby due in a few weeks, she preferred to believe his story to the effect that the killing had been unintentional. He had made a clandestine date with Frances at the river bank, ran his testimony. He had flourished the gun, but just to frighten her into promising secrecy about the pregnancy. She had grabbed at the weapon, and it had gone off accidentally during the ensuing struggle.

PREDATORY KILLINGS

Many a mother knows the experience of bringing home a newborn child only to find that an older infant becomes so jealous that he tries to strike the baby, or even hack at it with scissors or kitchen knife. Among juveniles as among adults, the emotional crime—dictated by jealousy, love, hate, fear or rage—need not occur in circumstances connecting it with sex. Nor does it have to take the form of murder.

Such crimes would differ from those detailed in the sex killings group only in that the damage inflicted would be less than death—or that the fuse of murder is lit by a circumstance other than sexual, as in the crimes of the rage killings group already examined.

But a quite different area of delinquency is that which encompasses crime committed in pursuit of robbery or other predatory gain. This type of offense, when attaining the point of murder, is easily recognizable. Two boys fatally "mug" a third in a hallway, so that they can steal his wallet. Or a nervous lad holds up a liquor store, someone moves, and out of sheer fright he shoots. Or again, a youthful car stealer is challenged by a motorcycle policeman. The boy steps on the gas. Pursued, he crashes into another car and kills three innocent people.

Such examples can be drawn *ad infinitum* from your daily newspaper.

It may be pointed out that the types of killings previously examined were preponderantly the work of children from fairly comfortable homes. Predatory killings, on the other hand, show a higher incidence of slum-raised offenders, of definitely under-privileged kids reared in squalor or want. The pursuit of money and what it represents is probably a prime instigating factor. This does not, however, rule out emotional considerations. The ends sought may be physical, as food—or psychic, as power. A child who owns a dozen balls still may swipe another from the candy store—just to see if he can. Here is a killing which took place under strongly predatory conditions; yet who is to say what actually motivated it?

Approximated from testimony and confession, the story goes thus:

The bus jounced along on the owl run of a freezing winter's night. Trying to avoid skidding, the driver kept his eyes on the sleet-blanketed avenue. Only two passengers riding—a skinny blonde in slacks, rather tall, and a shorter, stouter girl, shapeless in a thick overcoat.

Suddenly the driver felt something jammed into the small of his back.

A female voice said huskily: "Stop the bus and put up your hands."

The driver eased the heavy bus to the curb. He raised his hands and carefully turned.

The girl in slacks was pointing a gun at him. "Give the cash to her," she said, gesturing with the weapon toward the shorter girl.

The driver handed over his change belt.

"Now get down on your knees."

The driver had an impulse to grab the gun. Just a couple of kids. But why take a chance? The company was rich enough to stand the loss. He kneeled as ordered.

The tall girl said:

"How much did we get?"

"Thirty cents from the belt," said the other disgustedly, "and two dollars from his pockets."

"Is that all!"

"That's all I got, lady," the driver told her. "Only had a couple of other passengers tonight."

Without another word the girl pulled the trigger. Three times.

The man doubled forward, three slugs in his body.

The tall girl watched him for a minute as he writhed on the floor. Then she motioned to her companion and the two stepped from the bus.

The police caught up with them, a week or so later. An officer asked the tall girl why she had shot the driver.

She answered, quite calmly, "I just wanted to see if it would give me a thrill."

That self-analysis by our chilling murderess may or may not have been accurate. Anger and chagrin at the slim pickings probably helped pull the trigger. A contributing cause might have been predatory compulsion, or automatic precaution against later identification by the bus driver. She might have been showing her companion how tough she was. Or, as she says, she might have been merely seeking a thrill.

In any case, the killing again illustrates that classifying crimes through fortuitous association with robbery, sex or other factors—as being attempted here—while convenient, is purely arbitrary. The groups necessarily overlap and intermingle. Physical needs and psychic ones have been mentioned, but who can be sure where the physical stops and the psychic begins? Do not undernourished glands cause emotional disturbances, and vice versa? Only this much is certain—that every killing demonstrates *some* need; preternatural need, frustrated need, diseased need—and that when we become aware of it, we are too late. Murder has already been done.

The situation might be described thus: stimuli of all types cross the sensory threshold of the child, evoking responses. He sees an apple and wishes to eat it. But sometimes the responses are blocked, through flaws in the mechanism of the child or by environmental pressures. He cannot eat the apple because he is too small to reach it, or has no money to buy it. Multiply this frustration too often, add it to thousands of others, and we have a condition of severe need— not for the apple, particularly, but for closing the arc of response. It is as if electric current continues to flow into one plate of a condenser, building up an enormous potential. Finally the accumulation jumps the gap with a flash. The boy who never can reach the apple or any other fruit becomes frustrated, bad-tempered, aggressive—and takes it out on his companions.

One day he smashes the plate glass window and takes all the apples he wants.

Practically, then, the answer to juvenile murder is not to treat the offender after the spark has flashed, after the short-circuit has caused somebody's death. The barn door should be locked before the horse is stolen. If mental or physical flaws keep a boy hungry because he cannot respond normally to stimuli, let them be repaired. If environment constricts him, so that he cannot respond to satisfy his wants and needs, let the environment be changed, or weapons be given him to cope with it—or, in an emergency, let the wants be anesthesized.

But is all this possible?

Can the potentially dangerous offender be dealt with before he offends?

Apparently so.

We shall see in a later chapter that in the schools it is difficult to isolate the pre-delinquent or even determine delinquency's pre-disposing factors. Schools are teaching organizations, not analytical laboratories. But suppose the task were entrusted to properly equipped professionals? And suppose they did not look for causes of delinquency as such, but treated indications of *any* blocked or faulty responses—of *all* unfulfilled needs?

When this is attempted, encouraging inroads into delinquency can be made. Under this system, schools and other institutions dealing with children serve simply as sentry posts. Whenever they notice a child with markedly exaggerated behavior difficulties they refer him to a central agency, which analyzes the trouble and treats it. The agency may use its own therapists and facilities, as in the case of the Child Guidance Bureau operated by the school system in New York City. Or it may rely largely on cooperating facilities and practitioners in the community, as in the case of the St. Paul experiment—the pilot project of the kind.

The St. Paul (Minn.) idea was to organize church, charity, welfare and other local agencies, public and private, into a single mechanism to deal with delinquency by handling it in the incipient stages. A coordinating center was set up by the U. S. Children's Bureau, with the cooperation of the various local agencies. Referrals were made by welfare and church groups, schools, juvenile courts and police to the coordinating center, which would in turn determine the proper treatment for the child and refer him to the local agency which could provide it.

Referrals did not have to be on the basis of overt or serious delinquency. The emphasis, on the contrary, was simply on behavior symptoms. Thus, the coordinating agency sought any child who showed exaggeration of the following long list of behavior items:

Bashfulness
Boastfulness
Boisterousness
Bossiness
Bullying
Cheating
Cruelty
Crying
Daydreaming
Deceit
Defiance
Dependence
Destructiveness
Disobedience
Drinking
Eating disturbances
Effeminate behavior
  (boys)
Enuresis
Fabrication
Failure to perform
  assigned tasks
Fighting
Finickiness
Gambling

Gate-crashing
Hitching rides
Ill-mannered behavior
Impudence
Inattentiveness
Indolence
Lack of orderliness
Masturbation
Nailbiting
Negativism
Obscenity
Overactivity
Over-masculine be-
  havior (girls)
Profanity
Quarreling
Roughness
Selfishness
Sex perversion
Sex play
Sexual activity
Shifting activities
Show-off behavior
Silliness
Sleep disturbances

Smoking
Speech disturbances
Stealing
Stubbornness
Sullenness
Tardiness
Tattling
Teasing
Temper
Tics
Timidity
Thumbsucking
Truancy from home
Truancy from school
Uncleanliness
Uncouthness
Underactivity
Undesirable com-
  panions
Undesirable recreation
Unsportsmanship
Untidiness
Violation of traffic
  regulations

Of course, many of the listed items, no matter how marked in the individual youngster, may appear trivial, hardly to be construed as possible precursors to delinquency. Also, some are questionable on other counts: for instance, a given amount of sex activity may be abnormal behavior for one boy but quite normal or even sub-normal for another. Nevertheless, the list serves to illustrate the range and complexity of behavior disturbances, which, if allowed to fester, may result in juvenile crimes as hideous as any committed by adults.

In Chicago, in 1946, a triple murder came to light well demonstrating the issue.

It concerned William, a 17-year-old sophomore at Chicago University:

In June, the police caught up with William in a North Side apartment not far from the home of 6-year-old Suzanne, who had disappeared some six months before. A ransom note had been left behind, bearing fingerprints. The fingerprints were found to match William's.

During the arrest, a flower pot fell on William's head, perhaps assisted in its flight by one of the arresting officers. William feigned delirium for three days. He then confessed to having got rather drunk at school one evening. "It came into my head to go out." He went east, and seeing a window open in Suzanne's home, decided to burglarize the place.

Entering, he found himself in her room. She stirred in her sleep, and as he moved about, awoke. He strangled her. For reasons unclear to him, but perhaps to remove the only evidence of murder, he dragged the child's body to the basement, where he dismembered her in a bathtub. Outside, while dropping the pieces into a sewer, a manhole cover fell on his hand and he suddenly seemed to awaken. "It came into my head that I had done something wrong." He climbed back into Suzanne's room and wrote the ransom note, warning her parents not to notify the F.B.I. He thought this would delay search and for a time prevent the police from coming after him.

He confessed also that a few days later he climbed a fire-escape ladder and let himself into the apartment of Frances, a Wave. He stated he did not intend to rape her, but merely to steal what he could find. But Frances happened to be at home. She screamed. He shot her, and mangled her body with a knife.

William next confessed that a couple of weeks before his arrest he had slashed and strangled a 43-year-old divorcee. She had surprised him during burglary of her apartment.

The harrowing confession was so unbelievable, and

William himself so queer, that police took him to the scene of each crime with instructions to reenact it. This he did to their satisfaction, and seemed to enjoy it. But in each case there was a period of apparent amnesia. He remembered climbing to Frances' fire escape and killing her, for instance, but could remember no blood or anything else except waking some time later on the floor of her apartment. He recalled the older woman's excitement on seeing him, and his ramming of the knife into her throat, but could recall nothing more.

In jail, William spent most of his time praying.

He explained to investigators that he got no sexual satisfaction from the slayings, but did achieve it through the burglaries.

Observation revealed him a marked case of split personality of the Dr. Jekyll and Mr. Hyde type. His bad self he called "George Murman." He knew that George was a concoction of his own imagination, created about three years before, but he said, "George is very real to me."

The exact motivations and personality quirks behind this horrifying series of murders would be difficult to unravel. But whatever their nature and cause, they did not appear all at once, materializing, as it were, out of thin air. They developed from obscure seeds, like a cancer, until finally they drove William to kill. They grew out of repressions, disturbances, deep and unsatisfied needs; and while not necessarily pathological in the beginning, these must have manifested themselves in eccentricities of the type listed by the St. Paul experimenters.

By taking note of such early maladjustment and subjecting it to treatment, the St. Paul project made a start at locating and curing potential neurotics, psychotics—and juvenile murderers.

6

St. Paul and Stealing

THE ST. PAUL EXPERIMENT, COMMENCING IN 1937 and continuing for five fruitful years, marked a radical advance in the approach to delinquency. Famous among welfare and guidance people, its lessons, nevertheless, remain largely unknown to the public at large.

To understand the St. Paul idea, we need only examine a pair of cases chosen at random from those published by the supervising authority.

ANDY

In the eighth grade at school, tall Andy at 15 was somewhat shy with girls, perhaps because of his poor complexion. He wished he knew more about sex. His quest for information and outlet led him to indulge in sex play with younger boys, and finally he was reported to the police.

Ordinarily, he would have been hauled into Juvenile Court. For the first job of the police is to protect the community—and any repetition of the offense would have subjected them to criticism.

But thanks to the St. Paul experiment, a community service for children was available, to which they promptly referred the erring boy.

A case worker was assigned to help Andy, and first visited his home to find out if the seat of the trouble lay there. It did. Serious tensions were found to exist between Andy's mother and father, between the mother and Andy. A check with the Bureau of Catholic Charities revealed that these economic and emotional tensions were of long standing. But the mother's personality was such that little could be done about correcting the home situation. The case worker would have to concentrate on Andy himself.

71

Noticing that Andy had few recreational resources and could find little to do other than play with his father's electrical tools and think about sex, the case worker made contact with the YMCA, which invited the boy to a party. This experience caused him to join a neighborhood club, where wholesome, supervised recreation was to be had. Next, psychological tests revealed that Andy should have been doing better at school. Tutoring was arranged in arithmetic and reading. Andy could not do much with the arithmetic, but in three months his reading improved two grades! His interest in reading grew much stronger, providing him with another effective resource for recreation and self-improvement.

Most important of all, Andy finally agreed to see "the doctor"—a psychiatrist.

He found that the doctor spoke to him about sex as if he were an adult! He reciprocated by giving his side of the sex incident. This man was a real friend, a fellow you could talk to like you couldn't talk to your own father! He gave Andy the sex information he needed, touched on methods of self-control, helped him understand what society expected of him.

Further interviews followed. The psychiatrist was able to report to the police that any repetition of Andy's sexual offense was extremely unlikely.

As a matter of fact, no repetition occurred. In time, thanks to the continued effort of the community service, Andy made a normal adjustment, found an acceptable place in society. This might never have happened but for the help he had received in his school work, his recreation, and his personal sex problem. If this help had not been forthcoming, Andy could have developed into a dangerous delinquent. For reprimand or correctional sentence by the court could have scarred him for life, intensifying the very disturbances which had got him into trouble in the first place. . . .

Despite the encouraging tone of the report, all is not as well with Andy as it might be. At the time the project ceased its work, he was seriously embroiled in quarrels and tensions centering around his mother. He had quit trades school prematurely. Although for the moment he was happy in a part-time job, trouble might ensue from signs of rebellion the psychiatrist thought he could detect in him. But unquestionably he had been greatly aided, even if he would never come to as favorable terms with life as the boy in the next case.

For Andy came to the attention of the community service after overt delinquency had appeared. The St. Paul experimenters at first found it difficult to persuade cooperating agencies to refer children at an early enough stage, when behavior problems initially showed themselves. When this was done, as in the case which follows, the project's work proved easier and more effective. Potential delinquency was truly nipped in the bud.

RALPH

Here was a boy not yet delinquent or seriously misbehaved, and who might never become so. Yet at school he was showing some danger signs. He had always done poor work, but that was excusable, since his parents and teachers considered him rather retarded mentally, and he himself figured that he was "pretty dumb." The thing was that he had never seemed to care whether his work was good or bad. He made no effort to do better, which irritated his teachers and got him into trouble with them. Now he was doing even worse work. He took no interest at all in what was going on in class.

When teachers talked to him he stood silently, smiling.

The community service, after Ralph had been referred to it by the school principal, found itself puzzled. Investigation showed him to be the second of five children, who got along well together. The other kids were all quite bright and excellently adjusted. Ralph's father was a good provider who loved his family, and a quick and clever person. The mother proved stable emotionally, with a warm personality that resulted in ample feelings of support and security on the part of her children.

Why should Ralph, then, prove to be a behavior problem at school?

The answer was provided by a psychologist to whom Ralph was referred. Prolonged testing indicated that the boy was not mentally retarded at all; his intelligence lay between high-average and superior! He showed particular talent for art. But Ralph was less of an extrovert, less demanding, than his brothers and sisters. He had not seemed to shine beside them, and his parents had paid less attention to him. When the same characteristics caused Ralph not to do too well when he first began school, they immediately concluded he might not be up to par intellectually, and their attitude communicated itself to him. Ralph figured that his parents ought to know. Okay, so he was thick. He might as well not even try. When intelligence and other grading tests were given him later, he made no effort to do well.

Ralph's confidence in himself was restored—not so much by the psychologist's findings, but by the new attitude they created in his teachers and parents.

Special arrangements were made for him to catch up in his studies.

His behavior problem disappeared. . . .

The St. Paul experimental project, organized in the form of a community service for children, opened new pathways toward using existing community facilities. It concentrated on identifying and treating behavior problems before they could develop into serious delinquency and chronic personality disturbance. Its attitudes, knowledges and findings it passed on to other agencies important in controlling delinquency, such as the school and the police, thereby helping them meet the problem more effectively. It was frankly experimental, elastic and ready to improvise; and it operated in a limited area of the city.

How well it succeeded may be judged from the following tables (from the Children's Bureau publication, *Children in the Community*).

The yearly figures are reduced to an index number for easy comparison:

I. *Table showing number of boys arrested in project area as compared with the number arrested in the city at large**

Year	Project area		City of St. Paul	
	Number	Index	Number	Index
1937.............	161	100	1,547	100
1938.............	159	99	1,603	106
1939.............	120	75	1,857	120
1940.............	100	62	1,672	108
1941.............	136	84	1,994	128

* Data from St. Paul juvenile police division

II. *Table showing number of cases reaching Juvenile Court from project area compared with number from Ramsey County (St. Paul)*

Year	Project area*		Ramsey County**	
	Number	Index	Number	Index
1937.............	52	100	462	100
1938.............	30	58	405	88
1939.............	25	48	481	104
1940.............	18	35	510	110
1941.............	20	38	458	99

* Data from Ramsey County Probation Officer
** Data from Ramsey County Juvenile Court Statistics

III. *Table indicating effectiveness of treatment*

Effectiveness of treatment	Improvement in factors affecting behavior		Improvement in behavior		Improvement in either or both	
	Number	Per Cent	Number	Per Cent	Number	Per Cent
Total cases.........	404*	100	406	100	406	100
Major improvement......	17	4	66	16	71	18
Partial improvement......	260	64	254	63	265	65
No improvement.........	127	32	36	21	70	17

* Two cases did not seem to warrant judgment on basis of available evidence.

. Now the table on effectiveness of treatment applies to a whole gamut of behavior problems—not solely pre-delinquency or delinquency problems. Limited to the latter, treatment would have shown less success on the average, if only because in each case specific delinquency factors would have been already entrenched.

Further, the St. Paul method could be expected to avail little against a number of prominent types of delinquency; gangsterism, for instance, with its base in mob rather than individual psychology.

Nor would it help much against rural delinquency. Out in the corn belt, no close-knit marshalling of a broad variety of community services is possible.

Lastly, the experiment was purely local. What might work in St. Paul might fail in St. Augustine, where police organization, welfare conditions, services available, ethnological and cultural backgrounds of the population, are all quite different.

So the system of attack indicated in St. Paul is far from the answer to delinquency. Yet somewhat parallel findings by the Judge Baker Clinic in Boston, the Child Guidance Bureau in New York and various other agencies have confirmed the usefulness of coordinated catharsis of early disturbances. In the previous chapter it was suggested that conceivably such prophylaxis could stave off murder. Certainly it seems just what the doctor ordered for certain minor delinquencies on the style of misbehavior at school, truancy, running away and the like. To wit:

For more than two months, puckish Donald, 15, had fooled the Lake County officials. Picked up while wandering the streets of Evansville, Ind., late at night, he first told Probation Officer Walter Hammond that he could remember nothing except having been a hobo for a long time. He then said he was an orphan from Gary, Ind. Next, he concocted a story about his parents having been killed in an auto accident. Since he would not give his real name, it was difficult to check on him, and he was placed temporarily in a detention home at Crown Point.

He managed to escape. He got all the way to Calhoun, Ga., before police caught up with him and returned him to Crown Point. By this time, Lake County authorities had learned that Donald was a refugee from the Chicago Parental School.

It turned out that he had escaped from that institution and two others. He had been institutionalized after running away from no less than six foster homes! In all, Donald had been fleeing for five years, traveling through fifteen states!

The boy was identified by a relative of his step-father who came down from Chicago. "I wish there were something I could do," she said. "But he's incorrigible. He must have his father's wanderlust in him . . . his father just up and disappeared about ten years ago, after he and Don's mother were divorced."

Donald's mother remarried, but died a few years later. Donald was assigned to foster parents, and it was then that he began his series of flights. "You know, he's bright, and not basically bad," reported Officer Hammond. "He needs to be kept busy and given something to interest him. He needs strict discipline to keep him under control, too. But not a correctional institution. Unfortunately, like most states, we don't have just the place for him."

Donald did no display much affection for the relative who identified him. Asked why he always ran away, he replied: "I don't know, but I was always looking for some place to run to. Somewhere there is a nice place. I just know it."

He was told that he would be returned to Chicago juvenile authorities, but showed no reaction. Asked to promise that he would not run away again, Donald said nothing, just rubbed his eyes with grimy knuckles.

Donald's case, though an extreme one, seems to cry out for the St. Paul treatment! At any point in the saga, perhaps through coöperating community agencies a proper home might have been located for him. If not, he would have been strengthened and guided in adjustment to whatever home he did find himself in. Also, the community service could have diagnosed his special difficulties, and recommended the indicated handling to local correction officers or foster parents. If he had come to the attention of such a service immediately after his first runaway, possibly all the wasted years that followed would have been avoided.

But what of other categories of delinquency, more damaging to society than Donald's? Stealing, to name one. Do the St. Paul and similar experiences offer anything of value in combating unlawful acquisitiveness?

Stealing in one form or another—ranging from petty peculation to grand larceny—comprises our fourth major classification of child crime. It engages a greater number of children, perhaps, than any other of the serious delinquencies. The more or less standard type of armed robbery would go something like this example from Brooklyn:

Their high school classmates were astounded to learn that two students, Barry and John, had put across quite a crime wave. Police arrested the two 17-year-olds on charges of having staged ten stick-ups in four days, for a net of $1,500.

"I could give you 10 to 30 years in Sing Sing," Judge Samuel Leibowitz told the pair. "But I'm giving you a break." He sent them to Elmira on indeterminate sentences depending on good behavior and success of retraining.

The boys thanked him, saying that they had learned their lesson. "When you get to the Elmira Reception Center," advised the judge, "sit down and write a letter to each of your victims, telling them how you feel about a career of crime."

Girls, too, can get pretty rough, indulging in armed robbery and emulating the sluggings and muggings practiced by male guerrillas. In Albany, recently, three girls aged 14, 15 and 16 respectively were arrested on complaint of a 56-

year-old man. Two girls had lured him into an alley, he reported, where a third had "mugged" him, grabbing him around the neck from behind. Then the first two girls kicked his legs out from under him, and went through his pockets while he was lying on the ground.

Such thuglike methods are not rare among girl thieves, especially in our larger cities. But, as to be expected, most young ladies prefer less violent banditry. Statistically, shoplifting and purse-robbing are the most common forms. The girl in this account from a Boston newspaper has thousands of sisters all over the country.

The press of rush-hour crowds in the Park Street MTA was a thing of joy to a teen-aged South End lass. Today police believed they had discovered the reason—and it wasn't psychiatric. They claim that she is gifted with feather-fingers, and has taken advantage of the crush to open the handbags of at least 11 women.

Last night, the police charge, she filched a wallet containing $45 from a woman's handbag. This sort of thing might have gone on forever, but while monkeying with her victim's handbag the thief dropped her own. It contained $6, and papers which led to the girl's arrest.

The instances given thus far, occurring within a few weeks of each other in 1949, concerned adolescents. Many prior incidents illustrate that purse-snatching, at least, can be more precocious. Thus, in Atlantic City, N. J., the arrest of five girls aged 10 to 12 solved a puzzling series of purse thefts. The children had been operating all summer on the resort's bathing beaches, waiting until bathers would leave the sand for a dip, then rifling their pocketbooks. Scores were victimized, yielding cash and jewelry in excess of $1,500.

Another case from Boston, a burglary, has its lighter side. It seems that a teen-ager, caught under suspicious circumstances in a South End market, complained to police that he had bumped into an older competitor upon entering the building. "Who are you, a cop?" demanded the youth. "No, you fool," replied the other. "I'm a burglar. Go find your own place to rob." After some argument, it was decided to go over the place jointly. But as the police were arriving, according to the youth, the man fled, "leaving me alone without divvying up."

Either this lad was a colossal liar, as delinquents often are, or he was one of the almost countless number of wayward kids victimized by older criminals. Such victimization, however, usually is by a "fence" or other behind-the-scenes operator who uses children as cat's-paws. A representative affair concerns the proprietor of a candy store:

> Receiving stolen goods was the actual charge. Detectives had been suspicious for some time, but were unable to pin anything on him until one day a drugstore in the neighborhood reported itself looted of soap. The missing soap bars were found in his establishment, in the company of a 10-year-old boy. Questioning implicated two other boys, one 12, the other 14, as participants in robbery.

> Investigation brought out that this man had been making a practice of assigning children to steal from five-and-ten-cent stores, drugstores and chain groceries. No matter how high the value of the pilfered item, he would usually pay a penny or two for it, although on several occasions he had been known to pay a nickel.

Family and friends, when of criminal tendencies, can also be the Fagins using kids as dupes. In Ozone Park, L. I.— definitely a "better class" neighborhood—police arrested the mother of three for selling a revolver to a 15-year-old boy. Her own 15-year-old son connived in the sale. The two taught the purchaser how to handle the weapon and gave him other interesting information, apparently in hope of sharing in his loot.

Yet child thieves can get by perfectly well without leaning on their elders. Indeed, with independence and resource which would be most commendable if put to other use, adolescents can come up with projects as elaborate as this:

A park attendant noticed that shortly after dawn every day a trio of youths would enter the public lavatory to wash up. On his tip, detectives followed them one morning, walking a mile and a half to a spot under Paerdegat Basin Bridge, part of Brooklyn's belt parkway system. There the boys seemed to vanish into the ground.

Searching carefully, the detectives finally located their quarry in an extraordinary hideout—a huge cave under the bridge.

This hole burrowed into the sands of Canarsie, hidden from all eyes and "large enough to hold a hundred men," was well stocked with canned goods and tea. Here for many weeks the three boys had been living—on the proceeds, the detectives charged, of $6000 in stolen jewels. At the time of arrest, it was stated, the lads had been induced to dig up a chamois bag containing $3000 worth of jewelry not yet disposed of.

Of the three, Robert, 18, and Joe, 17, were arraigned on burglary charges. The remaining boy, a 14-year-old, was held for Children's Court investigation.

It was said that in their catacomb the lads had been living like feudal brigands, now and then throwing wild parties for friends and retainers. Among these, police located two 17-year-olds accused of selling a revolver to the 14-year-old, who had presented it to Robert.

What can be gathered from these several examples of the thousands of cases of juvenile sneak-thievery, burglary, robbery, minor extortion, shoplifting, picking pockets, and petty and grand larceny which make the records each year? As presented, bare of background, they tell almost nothing. Generalization from the mere physical facts of a crime is always dangerous. Even with fairly complete information, experts can be led into error.

For a long time it was assumed, for instance, that poverty was the one great cause of stealing. The more recent view is that this holds true only with respect to the pettier categories; when it comes to burglary, armed robbery, larceny in the upper brackets and other crimes yielding sizable plunder, a majority of offenders come from homes not impoverished. Similarly, there is less chance for petty thievery in rural communities; but farm and small-town boys are a match for dead-end kids at major pillage . . . and up and down the Middle West has run a tradition of countryside banditry, from Jesse James to John Dillinger, still showing itself in the juvenile crime percentages.

Yet all farm boys do not steal, nor city ones either. To get at the genesis of the juvenile thief, we must abandon the general in favor of the individual, peering, if we can, into the particular personal circumstances of each offender. Here is a case investigated by the New York *Journal-American:*

Described as a "svelte brunette from a Park Ave. home," 16-year-old Mabel had been arrested for cashing 18 worthless checks in various parts of the city. *Mabel states that she did it to embarrass her father, "who always ignored me in favor of my older sister." She hates him so much that she kicks the floor as she speaks of him. "As soon as you let me out, I'll start passing checks all over again!"*

Here is another:

After a series of 12 armed robberies in Brooklyn and New York, police finally caught up with tough, thin Frank, 14 years old. He confessed his crimes, offering no excuses. The investigator's report read in part: *"Frank . . . is one of 23 children his mother has borne to 6 different men, only the first of whom she ever married. He is living with his mother, his 2 half-sisters and his half-sisters' 6 illegitimate children."*

A third specimen case began when Marion, at 14, ran away with some other girls to Augusta, Ga., a thousand miles from her home city. She told Augusta authorities she was 17, whereupon they insisted she find work or leave town. She did neither. Marion was sentenced to jail. Some eleven days later the Travelers Aid Society secured her release and paid her way back.

But Marion did not return at once to her parents. She wandered about town on her own until, reported as "suspected of shop-lifting," she finally decided to go home.

In less than a year, she again ran away, this time being picked up by police in New York's Pennsylvania Station. Children's Court put her on probation. She joined a gang of adolescents preying on local merchants, and soon had the police trailing her in connection with a shoe store robbery. Sentenced to a year at the Hudson Training School for Girls, her conduct won her a parole. But she renewed acquaintance with the gang, and shortly afterward was again suspected of stealing.

Then one day, with another young girl, she badly pummeled two women and stole the purse of one—net proceeds, $11.50. As the youngsters fled, two youths came by and chased after them. Marion wound up in County Court, kicking and scratching so viciously that it took three male attendants to hold her. The judge gave her a year in the reformatory.

"Marion's parents are janitors in a tenement," read the probation report to the court. *"Her father is cruel, and her mother drinks. They live in a vermin-infested apartment. Marion would share one room with 3 of her sisters. Her brother, 15, is in the New York Training School, having begun as a housebreaker at the age of 12. Her 7 other brothers and sisters live unsupervised, the home filthy and dirty, and they poorly kept."*

These were the "particular personal circumstances" of Marion, according to the report, at the time she first left home.

No wonder she ran away! Any girl of spirit might be expected to. And if a lady too young to find work easily, and poorly motivated toward labor anyway, should decide to make a living by stealing rather than some other things she could think of—well, is it surprising? Anything was better than staying at home.

Once the ice was broken, once Marion began to steal—a

habit pattern formed. And whom could she find for companions but other kids who stole? Her own spirit—and her
first transgression—led her to almost unavoidable disaster.

As with Marion, so with Mabel, the chic and wealthy
check-passer, and with Frank, the child slum-bandit. In
each case, something was wrong, very wrong, in the family
circle. Such disturbances almost inevitably show themselves
in early behavior symptoms, in the school, in the street. But
nobody bothered to do anything about them. They were allowed to sprout into problem behavior, then delinquency.
It follows that something can be said for bringing all the
forces of the community to bear on early behavior difficulties—as in the St. Paul project!

Fine. So we are back in St. Paul. But suppose early behavior warnings are so slight as to be missed, or do not present themselves at all. Does the same approach work? The
answer is that if the original delinquency, great or small, is
treated before it has settled into habit, fair chances for correction still remain. A report from the St. Paul records
shows how an actual first case of stealing might be handled:

JERRY

At 9, this tot was picked up with some other boys stealing trinkets from a department store. The police avoided
formal complaint against one so young, and the St. Paul
service took over.

It was learned that both his mother and father were in
poor health. Further, they were nervous and highly excitable people. When a worker from the city's Child Welfare
Department called on them, the father promised that he
would severely punish Jerry so that he would not steal
again, but would the worker please not come back because
it would only make his wife excited and uncontrolled,
maybe hysterical?

It was decided on this and later evidence that to attempt
to help Jerry through his family would be futile. What about
school? The case worker found that he had good ability,
that he was somewhat retarded in reading, but not seriously.
But he was over-active and erratic, and unpopular with his

classmates. He always seemed to feel uneasy—and, he told the case worker, he now thought he knew why. A few days before he had done something to annoy his father, and in an angry, emotional outburst the father had let fall that Jerry was an adopted child. It was following this disturbing revelation that he had let some kids talk him into going with them to steal—not that he wanted the stuff, or that he didn't know it was wrong.

Investigation showed that Jerry was the illegitimate child of a relative. Illegitimacy in the family always gave acute shame to his "parents." They had raised Jerry as their own, shielding him from outside hurts and criticisms, but greatly demanding and over-critical of him themselves. To the case worker all this seemed to add up to the fact that Jerry, with the sensitivity of children, had felt not quite wanted at home. The insecurity had carried over into his classroom behavior. And after finding out that he was adopted, thus confirming his suspicions, he had gone along with the gang just to feel that someone was on his side, that he was accepted.

Evidence accumulated to corroborate the case worker's analysis. Take the day she visited Jerry in class. Unlike the other children, he did little work while she was there, but made every effort to attract her notice. He seemed desperate for attention, for friends, for people who would completely accept him and with whom he could discuss the many things bothering him. She arranged to meet the boy often. . . .

The report does not end here. But no need to go into the group work and other therapeutic devices arranged for Jerry's benefit. The point is that through the community service and cooperating community specialists in psychology, case work, group treatment and whatever else was required, Jerry's disease had been diagnosed and cure made possible.

What used to be the automobile age is rapidly becoming the air age, with youths today as willing to joyride in the upper atmosphere as on concrete. Of course, this brings the lads new problems. Planes are more difficult to get away with than cars. But on at least one occasion, juveniles pulled the trick. Their prize was a gorgeous two-engined job, formerly the property of the late General George Patton.

Flown to a New York airport after the war from the general's old Third Army base in Georgia, the plane had been sold to a civilian. Two neighborhood youngsters couldn't stand the strain of seeing the great bird lying idle.

One day they got a rifle somewhere and a few boxes of ammunition. Thus armed, and with a selection of sandwiches and candy, they sneaked into the plane and pulled a few likely looking switches. Managing to get it into the air, they flew it as far as Fairmont, Minn. There the gas gave out. They made a bellywhopper of a forced landing—and walked away unhurt!

Newspapers throughout the country, delighted with the story, made much of the two lads. Bold souls they, hardly to be considered delinquents!

Not so with kids who steal automobiles. These are delinquents indeed, eligible for charges of grand larceny.

In the United States, a car is stolen every three minutes. Auto theft is one of the commonest and most persistent of all crimes. Yet law officers ultimately recover more than 90 per cent of purloined vehicles; partly because few are stolen to be disguised and resold. Mostly they are taken for joyriding purposes, or to serve as expendable equipment in connection with other crimes—a man needs a car, and one not to be traced to him, when he wishes to make a getaway, rob a bank, run girls or heroin. As soon as the job is over he abandons it.

But it is in the joyriding department that junior excels. The spirit of adventure, the release and feeling of power which roaring horsepower can give, the love of machinery and chromium peculiar to American boys—these now drive lads of 21 or less to nearly half of all car thefts. They are exactly the motivations which made heroes out of the kids crazy enough to steal the Patton plane.

Where stealing for profit is the issue, your delinquent will not make off with the car. He will break into the trunk, remove parts or tires, sell them to the first junkman who will talk business. When it is the thrill of speed, of handling machinery, he is after—or a private place into which to retire with his girl—then he may yield to the temptation of an unlocked car door. His driving experience is limited, so as often as not he winds up in a wreck, as the Patton boys did. Sometimes he never gets started; as in this typical press story:

> A pair of 16-year-olds were charged with grand larceny today. They were captured by Detectives Thomas Tunney and James Green near Fourth St. and Main. The detectives said they noticed the boys try to enter several locked cars, and trailed them. The two got into the car of William Lloyd, 2 S. King St., and succeeded in getting it started by crossing the ignition wires. At this point the detectives stepped up.
>
> Both boys fled, despite warnings to halt. Tunney was obliged to fire a shot, striking one boy in the left side.

The latter incident occurred in one of our most crowded cities. Your small-town juvenile, when he feels the urge to step on the gas, like as not can borrow a jalopy from someone or steal his father's out of the garage for a few hours—if he does not have permission to use it. But to the slum boy a car represents something mighty remote, like a hundred-dollar bill or a cruise to South America. If he finishes school, and gets a job, and saves enough for a down payment, maybe someday he will have one. However, he may not prefer to wait that long. After all, he's not going to hurt the guy's car if he can help it. What harm in borrowing it for a while, ditching it when the gas runs out?

One "incorrigible" car thief, Harry, happens to be one of the best friends of the author, and this is said proudly.

For Harry, even as a lad, showed extraordinary qualities of loyalty, guts, and intrepidity. He did not do well in school, partly because he grew up in the shadow of an elder brother considered more endowed than he, which gave him a feeling of intellectual inferiority. But he had only one real fault. He was car crazy.

At 12, he stole his first one. The cops picked him up as he was teaching himself to drive. They let him off with a reprimand. A few days later they caught him fooling around under the hood of somebody's Studebaker. They brought him to the station house, but let him off again. Three months later, he was caught in an Oldsmobile with two other boys. This time it was the Family Court which let him off, probationed to his own parents. Two weeks later he was making off in a Buick when a prowl car gave chase. Harry blew a tire and wound up in the ditch. He presented such an innocent appearance in court, with his blue eyes and baby face, that the judge again let him go without sentence. It was on this occasion that the author got to know him, began to follow his case.

Harry admitted he liked to drive. It felt wonderful to step on the gas and zoom. But what really got him about a car was the motor. Did we appreciate what a motor was, he would demand time and again? Intricate, faithful, altogether lovely, much more so than human beings. Whenever he got the chance he would start taking a motor apart, just to caress the steel and see how the gadgets fitted together. He didn't know yet how to put the thing together again, but he was teaching himself; he would learn, all right. Maybe he would get a job in a garage after a while.

By the time Harry was 14 he had a record of stealing nine cars. He admitted privately to having "borrowed" others which the cops didn't know about. He had served a term in training school, where he made friends who found his loyalty useful. On the outside, he provided them with transportation. He was sent again to reform school, an upstate "farm."

This experience scared him. He was 17 now, and had no desire to spend the rest of his life in prison. No one would give him a job with his record, but his family, though disgusted with him, kept trying to help. His older brother now worked for a large corporation, and managed to get the boy an "office-boy" position with a friend in business.

Harry found the life dull, but stuck and worked hard. He was methodical and neat. The boss, though knowing his

record, deliberately entrusted him with more and more
responsibility. To let Harry know that he was considered
completely honest, he was assigned to handling money. For
many months, each Friday, he would run the firm's payroll
from the bank, quite alone.

But his prison friends kept looking him up, pestering him.
One day he showed up at the home of his boss, proudly inviting him to take a ride in his new car downstairs. Humor-
ing him, the boss went for a trip around the park. Two
youths, friends of Harry's, had been waiting on the back
seat and rode along. One of them confided to the boss that
the Mercury was "hot." A few weeks later Harry was found
in an automobile near a candy store which had just been
robbed by three boys. The car was not his. He claimed he
was innocent, but his record and the testimony of certain
unsavory companions who lived in the neighborhood were
enough to convict him of the store robbery as well as the car
theft.

This time he was put away for a considerable stretch at
a reformatory. There, as it turned out, he was assigned to
the auto shop. He was taught to assemble engines and repair them. He learned the use of tools and machining equipment.

On his release, he could not find a job. His parents staked
him to a set of tools, and he made a living by free-lance
repair work, pulling down cars in empty lots or in the
streets. Then he set up a small garage in a village some miles
out of town. This enabled him to get away from his prison
acquaintances. He had just begun to do pretty well, when
the war came. The Armed Forces would not accept him,
but on the recommendation of his parole officer, and with
special permission to leave the state, he was given a job in
a great airplane factory. Obliged to join a union, he found
himself with real companions for the first time in many
years, and worked hard at union affairs. His mechanical
skill, amounting almost to genius, was soon noticed. He
was given several raises.

After the war, the plant went back to making automobiles. Harry married a highly respectable girl, who bore

him a boy. At about this time, following a payroll robbery in New York, one of the armored-truck guards picked Harry's picture out of the rogue's gallery. Cops came to the plant and arrested him.

Bitterly protesting his innocence, Harry saw all his progress destroyed—or so he thought. The police had to release him. It turned out that at the time of the robbery he had been attending a union meeting in full view of several hundred persons! Shortly afterward, the plant appointed him to a supervisory post. The union elected him one of its officers.

Today, Harry is a perfectly respectable family man, fooling around to his heart's content with his kids—and with engines.

But what trouble and expense might have been saved the state—not to mention Harry—if someone had given him a set of tools and some cylinders to work on when he was 12!

7

Green Grow the Gangs

WIRY HAROLD, BETTER KNOWN AS "THE LITTLE Fox," had been caught off guard. And, it must be admitted, out of bounds.

At 16, he should have known better than to wander from his own block without adequate protection. A couple of "Bishop" guys jumped him and gave him his lumps.

You couldn't let them get away with it! Didn't they know he was a "Robin"? Anyhow, they were mooching around too close to home . . . Pretty soon they'd be walking in and taking over Robin territory.

The Robins declared war—formally inviting the Bishops to fight at a set time on a picked battlefield.

The Bishops accepted the challenge. And so it came about that one sultry evening in Brooklyn a group of less than a dozen Bishop boys slowly walked up the appointed street. They sidled cautiously to within a few yards of the waiting Robins, numbering half a hundred or more. Suddenly a Robin whipped out a "zip gun" and let fly. The handful of Bishops turned and ran. The whole Robin gang followed in whooping pursuit.

At the far end of the block, the Bishops melted into doorways. Brutal crossfire from roofs and cellars greeted the Robins. Ambush!

Raked by bottles, paving stones, garbage cans and .22 bullets, the Robins for a moment stood their ground, then backed away in stubborn retreat, fighting viciously. Bishops sortied into the street for hand-to-hand battle. At this point the police arrived.

They found only one boy killed—home-made guns don't shoot very straight, nor with much force beyond a few feet. But at least thirty or forty lads had been pretty seriously injured.

Police officers reaped a harvest of zip pistols, ammuni-
tionless German and Japanese guns, brass knuckles con-
trived from garbage-can handles, blackjacks, baseball bats
and knives of all sorts. They arrested seventeen boys, aged
12 to 16. And The Little Fox? Sent up for manslaughter. It
was he who had stabbed the dead Bishop.

So runs the typical juvenile gang episode. Its approximate
counterpart plagues the cities of America. From Michigan,
Missouri, Illinois, Ohio, Washington, California, Georgia,
Alabama and a host of other states the reports come in,
and from the District of Columbia. The mountain areas, the
coast sections, the North, the South—no part of the country
is exempt from at least sporadic outbreaks in the larger,
more urbanized communities. For gangsterism among youngsters is chiefly an urban problem. Its relative frequency
increases with concentration of population.

Now, we hear often enough that *all* delinquency tends
to increase with concentration of population. The author
wonders how much of the higher rate is simply a statistical
accident, arising for the more intensive policing and larger
number of children's courts available in crowded centers.
True, cities have delinquency-breeding slums—but farm
lands have delinquency-breeding hovels, and boredom.
However, if city delinquency does indeed outstrip its country cousin, we would estimate that it may do so solely by
virtue of the greater urban incidence of gangs.

Man is a herd animal. It is natural, and good, that he
should group, whether in the city or the sparsely populated
hinterlands. The child, on his own volition, begins to do so
at about the age of four. Early in man's history, perhaps so
early that he was still an ape or wore gills, he learned to
swarm for protection and convenience. But when one swarm
comes into conflict with another, it may become aggressive,
destructive.

Cultural differences—different languages, different social
habits, different economic circumstances, different patterns
of superstition with respect to the various colors and re-
ligions, are thrown together in our crowded cities, far more

than in open countryside, one stepping on the toes of the other. The result? Aggressive conflict between groups. Gangsterism.

Only in the public schools of certain northern and west coast cities, and here sparsely, is cultural separatism beginning to be attacked. Helen R. Faust, counseling specialist of the Philadelphia Public Schools, expresses it this way: "If educational planning includes delinquency prevention as an objective, special consideration must be given to tension areas."

Schools are the great levelers, the melting pots. Instances of school gangsterism, noted in an earlier chapter, have been noticed to decrease with elimination of color segregation—with increase in language comprehension as foreign-born rise through the grades—with more education in religious toleration—with greater efforts to integrate all individuals culturally into the school group.

Still, even in our most advanced clinics, the young gangster is being treated as an individual problem. "John? He desperately wants to be part of a group." "Joe is aggressive because he is frustrated, and being incapable of individual aggression, he joins a group of aggressors." "Mary sticks with a gang for a feeling of security."

All this may be true enough, as far as it goes, but it fails to bite into the heart of the matter. John wants to be part of a gang group because cultural differences cut him off from the major group—society. Joe is frustrated because he is black, or doesn't speak good English; culture isolates him. Mary feels insecure not because she is poor, but because most of the girls at high school won't accept anyone so badly dressed, so unkempt; in short, so culturally foreign.

Each is driven to flock with his own kind, inevitably coming into conflict with other kinds—including the main body of society. The tragedy is that the minor groups, quarantined, perpetuate their own little cultures—their own sets of prejudices, ignorances and habits. The vicious circle sharpens enmity. And associated feelings of persecution and envy make for revolt.

In New York, where the Robins and Bishops fought,

concentrations of population and variations in cultural background are numerous. As to be expected, its gangs are many and violent. Using them as prototypes to provide a rough picture of juvenile gangs everywhere, let us inspect their characteristics more closely.

Some estimates place the number of New York boy gangs at sixty. Others go as high as two hundred. These include only gangs which have come to the attention of police, probation officers and welfare workers. A count is difficult because the larger gangs have "seniors," "juniors," and young auxiliaries known by such names as "Tiny Tims." A loose system of alliances runs throughout the city, including, on occasion, hook-ups with adult thugs and racketeers. Membership may run anywhere from a dozen boys up to hundreds. If a list were to include organized gangs which had not yet come to the attention of the police, according to one prominent sociologist, Harlem alone would show 250 gang groups. When a 15-year-old "Black Hat" recently killed himself accidentally while preparing his zip gun for a gang battle, the Brooklyn district-attorney's office immediately put 32 gangs under investigation, naming them as follows:

Bedford-Stuyvesant section: Tiny Tims, Socialistic Gents, Nits, Robins, Little Vikings, Jolly Stompers, Imperials, Dillinger Boys, Buccaneers, Brewery Rats, Little Bishops, Beavers, Batchelors, the Decatur St. Boys and others.

East New York-Brownsville section: Black Hats, Bristol St. Boys, Musketeers, Comets, Bambinos, Fulton St. Boys and Gestapos.

Navy Yard section and Williamsburg: The Allies, Angels, Harpo Gang, Latin Counts and Comanches.

Manhattan and the Bronx boast their own extensive rosters of picturesquely named gangs. Queens and Staten Island, where populations are less concentrated and culture more homogenous, as yet show no gang problem.

About seven out of ten gangs are limited to boys of a particular persuasion, national origin or color. There are Negro gangs, Italian gangs, Jewish gangs. Sometimes the clannishness shows in the name: the "Irish Dukes" and "Puerto Rican Eagles."

The New York *World-Telegram* reports that gangs have a jargon of their own. *Session* means dance. *Sneaky Pete*— a mixture of port and sherry, or of either wine with gin. *On the bop*—on the prowl for street brawling. It is known that many gangs adopt identifying clothing or mannerisms. Robins wear blue hats with narrow bands; Beavers, black fuzzy felts. Comanches affect studded belts, useful in fighting. Some gangs walk in characteristic style, with a limp, a shuffle or drooped shoulders.

The Comanches are one of those groups which have connections with adult gangsters who supply money, weapons and advice.

On one occasion they lent the youths six large automobiles for transportation to a street fight.

Typically, a feud between gangs unfolds itself as in the recent case of two Harlem gangs—the "Sabers" and the "Slicksters." Relations between them became so violent that the Homicide Bureau was compelled to take matters out of the hands of the Juvenile Aid Bureau, the police arm which usually deals with delinquency. First casualty was one of the Sabers, 15-year-old Joseph, fatally stabbed with a bayonet, an ice pick and a "commando" knife. Sabers retaliated by attacking a large group of Slicksters on Lenox Avenue, and—with exactly the same trio of weapons—doing to death Victor, also 15. Next morning another youth was found stabbed at 9 A.M., fifty feet from the high school for which he was bound to attend classes. During one of the clashes, a girl was wounded by a .22-caliber bullet. In court, the assistant district attorney complained, "Each of these youthful gangs has its membership graded according to age as Tiny Tims, kids, cubs and seniors." He accused suspects of using daggers, bayonets, ice picks—along with revolvers and what he officially called "zipper guns."

Where in the world do children get hold of firearms?

According to police and city probation officers, one source is the reservoir of souvenir guns brought home by war veterans. Sometimes the youngsters wheedle or "borrow" them from older brothers. More often they appropriate them in the course of house-breakings and burglaries.

Should money come the way of the youngster by pawning stolen articles or via the shakedown route, he finds it easy enough to purchase weapons at less-than-particular pawn-shops and through mail order houses—one of which extensively advertises its wares in comic books. Ammunition can be bought at sporting goods stores, or pilfered at amusement-arcade shooting galleries: "Instead of shooting off the whole gun load at the target, you just slip a few shells into your pocket." It is said that somewhere Brooklyn's Navy St. Gang got hold of a machine-gun and sold it to the Redskin Rhumbas for fifty dollars!

Home-made, however, are most guns used by the boy gangs. With the technical ingenuity characteristic of American youngsters, these lads think nothing of converting a toy cap pistol into a single-shot arm which will fire cartridges, nails or pins. Many fashion their weapons in trade school or high school shops, assembling them at home. Such jobs—consisting of wooden handle taped to metal tube, with a filed key to serve as firing-pin and rubber bands doing duty to spring the trigger—form the famous "zip" or "zipper" guns. They take .22-caliber ammunition.

"We can't stop kids making guns," states Brooklyn's Assistant District Attorney John E. Cone, "but we can try to control the sale of bullets." He adds, however, that such controls offer temporary relief at best. "We have to get at the source. Our only means . . . lots of plain, simple understanding."

But understanding is all too scant. The gang killings go on.

One alarming aspect of the situation is the growth of the girl gang. These first became prominent during the war, when they invaded the bright-light areas, lured soldiers and sailors into side streets where boy accomplices too young to be drafted would "roll" the uniformed men for their wallets. One court report tells of a Bronx gang which assigned girl members to waylay the leader of a rival Manhattan gang, lead him to a loft and seduce him. While the program was under way, the Bronx boys called the police, had the Manhattanite jailed for rape.

According to Bradford Chambers, a delinquency expert who made a survey of girl gangs at the time, they showed a low incidence of venereal disease and illegitimate births.

This still holds true. But in every other respect the situation has become worse since the end of the war. More girls are engaged in gangsterism; and they are committing crimes more severe. Gang offenses among girls between the ages of 14 and 17, in 1948 and the first six months of 1949, ran almost ten percent higher than during the peak-delinquency war year of 1943; but what police complain of most is that the girls are even more difficult to handle than the boys! Bronx magistrates call girl offenders more violent than ever before. Manhattan police state, "These junior gun-molls are tougher than the guys!" In Brooklyn, an emergency meeting in 1949, attended by magistrates, representatives of the district attorney, police officials and senior probation officers, emphasized that the adolescent girl gangster, in that borough, too, excelled her boy colleague in sheer viciousness.

Only rarely does the girl gang function without affiliation. In the great majority of cases it exists as the auxiliary of some boy gang, to which it gives fierce loyalty. One important duty, as described at the 1949 conference of Brooklyn law enforcement officers, is to act as weapons carriers to the boys, who thus escape seizure and charges. The girls also supply alibis, claiming that a suspect boy was with them at a "session" or in bed at the time of a crime's commission. Principally, however, the young ladies act as camp followers, supplying the lads with such sex as they require—and fulfilling duties as lures and spies.

These bands of girls go under such names as "Robinettes," "Chandeliers"—after a peculiar hair-do—and "Shangri-la Debs." They comport themselves viciously in street-fighting, although rarely using guns. A favorite weapon is the lye can and bottle of pop. When one girl slept with a boy member of an opposing gang, girls of her own group set out to punish her with the lye-and-soda mixture—detectives, fortunately, interfering before damage could be done. On another occasion, during a battle involving boy gangs and their respective auxiliaries, one tender lass hurled the mixture at a boy enemy. It missed him, struck a wall, bounced back, and horribly burned the girl's face, neck and shoulders. Another girl, a 15-year-old described in the press as "a pretty little miss, apparently sweet as the breath of heather," was in the habit of attacking with broken beer bottles. A week after being paroled for mashing up an 18-year-old girl with such a weapon, she was arrested with three child companions for beating a second girl, 16, with fists, kicking her in the stomach, burning her with cigarette butts.

The sex practices of these gangsterettes are particularly revolting. Homosexualism seems to be unknown, but any member over 12 is expected to give her favors to the boy gangsters. Older girls, to curry favor or by command, have been known to procure younger ones for the pleasure of their male gang leaders. One recorded case concerns a Manhattan girl, a Negress, caught by white girls in an East Bronx bailiwick. The girls dragged her to the cellar clubroom, where she was forced to submit to fourteen young mobsters.

Probation reports describe the initiation ceremony of the Shangri-la girls as requiring each neophyte to have intercourse with one of the boys of the Tiny Tim gang. Often girls thus initiated are no older than 12. It is said that the honor of performing the rite usually goes to a specific member of the Tiny Tims—known to his fellows as "Willie the Lover."

Judge John F. X. Masterson of Adolescent Court, attempting to awaken the public to action, recently released this story to the press:

A prospect was enthusiastic about joining a certain girl gang—until the induction ceremony was explained to her. Then she rebelled.

The recruiting agent and her friends promptly beat the girl, tied her up and proceeded to brand her chest with lighted cigarettes. They got as far as "Ei---" in their nasty little word game when the girl's screams scared her torturers off.

The sordid life of these degenerate girls stands well revealed in an incident which took place in the Bronx—at about the time the enforcement officers were holding their meetings in Brooklyn:

Warfare broke out between the "Comets" and "Happy Gents" at Claremont Community Center, P.S. 55, with the stabbing in the abdomen of Carl, a 16-year-old Happy Gent. From what police could learn, the trouble between the two gangs started when the Comets took some girl friends away from the Happy Gents.

The Comet leader, a 17-year-old, was held in $15,000 bail. He had a zip gun in his possession.

Others held included Leroy, arrested with a sawed-off carbine hidden in his trousers leg. He lived with one of the girls in the gang clubrooms. Another girl is expecting a baby fathered by one of the gang.

The Magistrate observed that gangster movies and comics were to some extent responsible for youthful gangs. He added about the arrested boys: "They come from substandard homes . . . possibly from the lowest rung of the economic ladder. Ultimately, I suppose, they will be sent to jail. That will be punitive action. What is being done about corrective action?"

One form of "corrective action" is the establishment of recreational and social facilities, based on a threefold idea. First, such facilities keep kids off the streets, where they get in trouble. Second, athletic and social events, such as dances, furnish thrills and excitement substituting for those otherwise sought in delinquent behavior. Third, a supervised environment is provided to make up for lack of home life.

It will be noticed, however, that the cited battle between the Comets and Happy Gents took place in a community recreational center.

All children have a right to play space and play facilities, and a society which deprives them of these by compressing kids into cities in all fairness should make replacement in kind. Further, juvenile play centers can sometimes serve ideally as settings for group work therapy. And in the over-all picture, when shrewdly conducted and adequately sustained, they will undoubtedly contribute their ounces of prevention. Nevertheless, recreation, itself, fails as a panacea. *Nowhere has any significant statistical relationship been shown between incidence of play facilities and incidence of child crime.* "Plenty of action at a club is not a cure for delinquency, but one kind of preventative medicine," says *The Child*, monthly report of the Children's Bureau, commenting on a pre-delinquency program advocated by West Virginia's Governor Clarence E. Meadows. And it is "preventative medicine" not because of recreational factors—but because the latter act as honey to attract the fly. Once within the center, the straying child must be given the full treatment of skilled analysis, guidance, control and social reconditioning—or he will stray again, and further.

Thus it often happens that the recreational center actually creates and fosters gangs! Gang groups have been known to take over the centers—physically—finding them superior headquarters to the usual cellar club, back room or empty lot.

In New York as in other parts of the country some gang organizations, it is said, have been rescued for society by means of social, athletic or other recreational clubs supported by individuals. Perhaps so. A few of these have done some good; the Abe Stark project in Brownsville is a well-known example. But for the most part these efforts turn out as abortive as they were well meant. For the problem is too complex for individual, non-professional handling—and generally too expensive. And when the sponsor runs out of funds, or finally admits he is getting nowhere, in either case closing the project's doors—its members stray back to gangsterism even more virulent than before.

Recreational centers sponsored by experienced private

with lighted cigarettes. They got as far as "Pi---" in their nasty little word game when the girl's screams scared her torturers off.

The sordid life of these degenerate girls stands well revealed in an incident which took place in the Bronx—at about the time the enforcement officers were holding their meetings in Brooklyn:

> Warfare broke out between the "Comets" and "Happy Gents" at Claremont Community Center, P.S. 55, with the stabbing in the abdomen of Carl, a 16-year-old Happy Gent. From what police could learn, the trouble between the two gangs started when the Comets took some girl friends away from the Happy Gents.
>
> The Comet leader, a 17-year-old, was held in $15,000 bail. He had a zip gun in his possession.
>
> Others held included Leroy, arrested with a sawed-off carbine hidden in his trousers leg. He lived with one of the girls in the gang clubrooms. Another girl is expecting a baby fathered by one of the gang.
>
> The Magistrate observed that gangster movies and comics were to some extent responsible for youthful gangs. He added about the arrested boys: "They come from substandard homes . . . possibly from the lowest rung of the economic ladder. Ultimately, I suppose, they will be sent to jail. That will be punitive action. What is being done about corrective action?"

One form of "corrective action" is the establishment of recreational and social facilities, based on a threefold idea. First, such facilities keep kids off the streets, where they get in trouble. Second, athletic and social events, such as dances, furnish thrills and excitement substituting for those otherwise sought in delinquent behavior. Third, a supervised environment is provided to make up for lack of home life.

It will be noticed, however, that the cited battle between the Comets and Happy Gents took place in a community recreational center.

All children have a right to play space and play facilities, and a society which deprives them of these by compressing kids into cities in all fairness should make replacement in kind. Further, juvenile play centers can sometimes serve ideally as settings for group work therapy. And in the over-all picture, when shrewdly conducted and adequately sustained, they will undoubtedly contribute their ounces of prevention. Nevertheless, recreation, itself, fails as a panacea. *Nowhere has any significant statistical relationship been shown between incidence of play facilities and incidence of child crime.* "Plenty of action at a club is not a cure for delinquency, but one kind of preventative medicine," says *The Child*, monthly report of the Children's Bureau, commenting on a pre-delinquency program advocated by West Virginia's Governor Clarence E. Meadows. And it is "preventative medicine" not because of recreational factors—but because the latter act as honey to attract the fly. Once within the center, the straying child must be given the full treatment of skilled analysis, guidance, control and social reconditioning—or he will stray again, and further.

Thus it often happens that the recreational center actually creates and fosters gangs! Gang groups have been known to take over the centers—physically—finding them superior headquarters to the usual cellar club, back room or empty lot.

In New York as in other parts of the country some gang organizations, it is said, have been rescued for society by means of social, athletic or other recreational clubs supported by individuals. Perhaps so. A few of these have done some good; the Abe Stark project in Brownsville is a well-known example. But for the most part these efforts turn out as abortive as they were well meant. For the problem is too complex for individual, non-professional handling—and generally too expensive. And when the sponsor runs out of funds, or finally admits he is getting nowhere, in either case closing the project's doors—its members stray back to gangsterism even more virulent than before.

Recreational centers sponsored by experienced private

welfare groups, rather than individuals, sometimes run into the same difficulties. Take the district of the Tompkins Park Neighborhood Council, affiliated with the Brooklyn Council for Social Planning, in turn associated with the New York Welfare Council, jointly supported by Protestant, Catholic and Jewish youth agencies. Surely this type of intra-city organization knows or should know, that basic to gangster-ism is cultural conflict. But for all its resources and skill, it meets great difficulty in curing delinquency—or at least gang delinquency—through recreational facilities. In the cited neighborhood, the director of the Lafayette Community Center is obliged to report fighting between a "white group and a Negro boy." A field worker for the Brooklyn Council investigates, and in turn reports:

> Supposedly, three nights before, a trio of Negro gangsters beat up a Puerto Rican boy. Next night, three white boys beat up one of the Negro boys.
> Then, on succeeding nights, the groups began to gather. Finally a group of 65 white boys threatened to rush the community center to seize some Negro boys. These whites were reputed to be the "Pulaski St. Boys." They were persuaded not to rush the building and left, threatening to return with more boys.

The Pulaski kids returned, all right. A battle ensued in the streets, according to newspaper reports. Though casualties were rumored plentiful, no check could be made—for as police arrived on the scene, the two factions scattered, taking their wounded with them.

In this type of incident, recurring so often in large cities the country over, can be glimpsed the origins of some of the rationalizations for gang behavior given by the boys themselves. "Hell, if you ain't with the mob, they'll break your neck." "If you ain't organized, how can you put them guys in their place?" "They'll get you, if you don't run with a gang of your own." "Sure I got a gun. The other guys got 'em. You want me to be shot?" "Ain't safe to walk around without a zip or knife and some friends." But the real explanation? Again—cultural tension!

When the recreational project is publicly operated—as by the schools or police—it might be expected to work more potently as a delinquency antidote, since it is backed by larger funds, greater authority, broader experience. This does not necessarily follow. Through inadequate personnel, through mistaken programming featuring amusement without accompanying cultural conditioning, or simply through running up against habits too deeply ingrained to be coped with except under institutionalized conditions, the center may fail to stem the tide, may actually stimulate it.

Brownsville's Black Hat gang, for example, began as a social club—a group project for boys showing behavior difficulties, organized by directors of the community center at a local public school. Directors recall that the boys didn't show enthusiasm for the group games—basketball, baseball. Never staying long at one activity, the boys would "wander aimlessly in and out of the school." One director states:

"Their only interest was in girls . . . not a particularly healthy interest at that. They played only rough-house, body-contact games. We were always afraid that they'd force one of the girls into a darkened classroom upstairs. We tried to watch them carefully."

The directors saw that the general recreational program was failing, that the boys were becoming greater troublemakers. It was then that the decision was made to organize them into a club. Three classrooms were assigned to them for meetings, which were attended at first by about 75 boys. Under supervision they behaved well enough, and began to develop a solidarity—solidarity among themselves, not with society.

Formal meetings dwindled in attendance, but the solidarity persisted. Remembering the tales of fathers and brothers who had come home from the war just a few years before, the boys organized themselves in military fashion. They formed four squads, the first being a "striking force of the best fighters," aged 18 and 19. The second squad was somewhat younger, known as "the brains." The third and fourth squads were comprised of 14- and 15-year-olds. Each squad had fifteen or twenty members. For a uniform, they settled on wearing black chauffeur's caps, hence the name "Black Hats." Soon some of the boys took to carrying zip guns, objectors being overruled. The gang began throwing its weight about, went out into the streets looking for trouble. They found it. Other gangs went "on the bop" for the Black Hats. A killing occurred, reported as an accident . . . and the rest of the story is written on police blotters.

Apart from the schools, the New York police operate a system of juvenile recreational facilities through the Police Athletic League. These are popular, but thousands are turned away from the limited gym and play areas available. Police, and particularly probation officers, in almost daily contact with the delinquency problem, often develop a practical approach which can yield excellent results if given a chance. An investigation of post-war delinquency by Robert H. Prall, in behalf of the Scripps-Howard newspapers, turned up the following case in point:

Two young Brooklyn probation officers, George Sable and Arthur Cohen, voluntarily took it on themselves to do what they could about the borough's rising delinquency rate. At Lafayette Community Center, in the heart of one of the trouble areas, they set up temporary headquarters and invited leaders of the various gangs to a meeting.

As probation officers, they had sufficient authority over some twenty-five such gangsters—all on probation—to get them to attend. These boys represented eight gangs. They did not greet or even look at one another. Officer Sable made a plea that the boys jointly agree to stop carrying knives and guns. They made no response, just sat silent and poker-faced. Then Officer Cohen suggested that introductions be made, and told Two-Gun Rocky, one of the leaders, to "stand up and take a bow."

Rocky rose, stood sheepishly. The others snickered. More boys were introduced. Again, snickers. Seizing the chance presented by this fleet change of mood, Officer Cohen said, "Look—settling a fight, you can always get your gun. But . . . if you get the other guy, the police get you. Or he gets you, and the police get him. Either way, both lose. Is that right?" Still more snickers, and a few giggles. Officer Cohen then suggested that arbitrators be chosen to adjust all disputes. "And if the board can't settle the argument, then we'll put on a trial by combat, like in the days of King Arthur, only with boxing gloves."

The boys stopped snickering. Officer Sable jumped up and said, "Trouble with you guys is that you're yellow!"

The young gangsters looked at each other. Yellow? Afraid of trial by combat? Afraid, as Sable further accused them, of trying anything new?

The two probation men left the room to let the boys discuss matters. When they returned, a leader known as "Booby" told them: "Okay. The Imperials will go along —if the other guys do." Slowly the rest fell into line. A board of arbitrators was picked.

After that, for several weeks, none of the accustomed gang delinquency occurred in the area. Then some of the leaders of the senior gangs reported that trouble was brewing among affiliated junior gangs. "We've lost control of them kids."

The probation officers quickly called meetings of the small-fry. They induced them to agree to arbitration. At the same time they warned senior leaders that they would be regarded as breaking probation if they allowed their juniors to step out of line. This kept the peace until a few days later, when members of the Tiny Tims and Little Robins, a pair of rival junior groups, walked into the probation bureau and pleaded for permission to fight. "One of the Tiny Tims hit a sister of a Little Robin. We ain't standing for it!" a boy told Officer Sable. He advised them to pick one member from each gang to settle the dispute with boxing gloves. But apart from the gang, the boys weren't so tough. They did not relish fighting as individuals. Before an hour had elapsed, a Little Robin reported: "We talked the whole thing over. It would be kinda silly to fight now. We're calling off the bop."

The probation officers continued to hold meetings at least once a month, at which gang disputes were settled through arbitration, or in the boxing ring. More and more gangsters attended these affairs. The officers knew enough to remain in the background, letting the boys' natural leaders conduct proceedings under unobtrusive guidance. They also knew enough to steer the conversation around to such topic as sex and racial discrimination, thus skillfully achieving a measure of both physical and mental hygiene. They saw to it that plenty of entertainment was provided at the center, including jazz bands.

Thus—by easing tensions between the gang groups, by attacking general cultural conflict, by rendering hygienic assistance and using recreational bait—the two probation officers without outside assistance achieved a result even they had not expected. Within six mon'hs, almost no arrests were being reported in the district for the typical gang offenses—assault, disorderly conduct, robbery, mugging, shakedown. This at a time when such offenses in the rest of the city continued at the "normal" rate, or showed increases.

But in all Brooklyn, one of the worst delinquency areas in the world, only seven probation officers work through Adolescent Court. They handle thousands of cases annually! Under the weight of such a load, Officers Sable and Cohen were obliged to give up their experiment. Before doing so, they arranged a conference of state probation officers, judges, a deputy police commissioner, assistant district attorneys, representatives of the school system and social agencies, ministers—and even one gang member. This work was important. It was getting results. Someone should continue it. "We thought the meeting would take up where we left off," says Officer Cohen. "But since that time there has been no concentrated effort from those sources to do anything about it. As a result, even the gangs with which we were successful have resumed their predatory activities. They are hoodlums again."

Once more the vital lesson: to make inroads into the city gang, the requirements are skilled leadership and a sustained program aimed at areas of tension. Recreational opportunities themselves are not sufficient—are not, perhaps, even essential.

In a climate of larger prejudice, tension and conflict,

smaller ones become inevitable—extending even to recreations and sports. Without basic correction, the athletic clubs themselves can degenerate into gangs, and often do. To illustrate, we cite court information about one slaying—typical of a number—which took place a few days before this was written:

The victim, Teddy, 17, was vice-president of the "Lightnings," a Bronx stickball team. Testimony is that seven members of the "Rockets," a rival team, chased him to Union Ave., where he was knocked down, kicked, beaten and stabbed. Five shots were fired. A passer-by was seriously wounded. A bullet still in the body will be checked against a .38-caliber revolver and a zip gun said to be owned by Rocket team members. Coroner reports that actual cause of death was a knife wound.

Managing to break loose during the fight, the victim jumped on the running board of a passing automobile, but collapsed on the way to the hospital. He died one hour later. Fifty detectives were assigned to the case. Thirty boys were rounded up and questioned, leading to arrest of five Rockets. The revolver was found on a rooftop, the zip gun in an alley; a knife was picked up later in the streets which a Rocket boy admits throwing away after the fight.

The quarrel began when a member of the Lightnings was struck by a batted ball, at about 3 P.M. The quarrel seemed to be smoothed over, but late that night the seven Rockets ambushed their victim as he was leaving a dance at Melrose House attended by various Lightnings.

gangs ravishing white women accused of sleeping with Negroes, and two of Negro girls accused of sleeping with whites. Or imagine the feelings of a group of frustrated, under-privileged, under-cultured and probably low-intelligence slum boys coming on an appetizing, expensively dressed lass —subjecting herself to her Lord Fauntleroy on a park meadow or in the back of a car. To them she may appear fair game—with sudden emotions of envy and resentment unquestionably entering into the beating given the boy-friend and the raping given the girl. Rape cases of this variety are routine on police blotters.

Marijuana has been blamed for adolescent joint-rapes both in New York and on the west coast, but the evidence is not reliable. Liquor, on the other hand, seems definitely to have been the inflammatory factor in three out of fourteen joint-rapes by juveniles in seven cities, reported in the past twelvemonth—and in six out of nine such cases in rural areas during the same period. Examination of eighty-seven cases over a ten-year interval in cities of New York, Pennsylvania and New Jersey leads the author to suspect that among urban boys the arousing circumstance is never, or hardly ever, a dance, petting party or other occasion of erotically stimulating contact. These provide their own outlets. If climax presses, climax arrives. On the other hand, out of seventeen rapes in the rural areas of the same states, fifteen occurred after dances or church socials. Perhaps the farm girls keep their boys at too great a distance.

One word more. Juvenile joint-rape is not a frequent crime. Many rapes of all kinds are listed by police departments as assaults, sometimes as sex crimes, often without clear indication of whether rape was accomplished or intended. It is difficult to arrive at reliable figures on the number of rape cases which reach court, let alone those which never do. Sex offenses of any kind serious enough for juvenile court notice, however, would seem to make up not more than eight percent of all delinquencies. Of these, less than two percent are rapes or near-rapes, with only a fraction of a percent being recorded as joint-rapes.

Even among the gangs of the great cities, which, like

wolves, do everything in packs, a type of morality, shame or caution makes boys rugged individualists when it comes to sex assault. Although the joint-rape does occur, it is not usually premeditated or pre-organized. We have no way of knowing whether poor Manya was ravished as the result of a habit of going to the roof in pajamas every night with her dog, so that she was noticed, and deliberately ambushed by plan. But the chances are that the rape was more or less spontaneous, a mob explosion dictated by fortuitous combination of opportunity and inflammatory circumstance.

The conditioning environmental factors must not be overlooked, however. The careful opinion of the author is that cultural tensions and distances create most juvenile mobs and gangs, including the raping kind. In New York, tension between Negroes and Puerto Ricans can explode into rape—in Texas and Calfornia, between Mexican and native-born—in New England, between Catholic and Jew. But the greater offending area is the South. In any given year, rapes of Negro girls by groups of white youths_ outnumber all juvenile joint-rapes in the rest of the country combined, by a ratio variously estimated at from 3 to 1 up as far as 10 to 1.

Much of what has been said about the joint-rapist applies to the individual one. But he is apt to be less a rapist. That is, some lady may entice him beyond his powers of resistance, and later—sorry, ashamed or pregnant—claim rape. Or she may tease more effectively than she knows, not realizing his low sex threshold. Often he is a fellow who wins a girl's consent, only to find that the law does not recognize her as old enough to know her own mind—or body. In which case, he may be charged with statutory rape.

But considering only ordinary rape—ravishment involving neither the encouragement nor consent of the girl—we find again that behind it stands some inflammatory circumstance. It may be a matter of coming on her when already inflamed by liquor, emotions or erotic environmental stimuli—or when she is in such state as to do the inflaming. She is alone. She is naked. She is drunk and helpless. She is feeble-minded, and won't know the difference. Or, as one psychiatric court worker wrote, "she symbolized the boy's unkind mother, and so had to be destroyed, though at the same time loved."

That inflammation which may rise from the girl's circumstances accounts in good measure for the rapes occurring in conjunction with other juvenile crimes. The adolescent second-story man is out for plunder, not sex. But he comes on a girl scantily clad, a woman in a scented bedroom. The situation is too much for him, especially if he happens to touch her in pursuit of jewelry or to subdue her. Lust pulls the trigger—and he rapes.

It is the adult—and psychotic—rapist who works the other way. He plans his attack primarily as sexual, stealing only as a secondary matter when opportunity presents itself, in order to keep himself alive for more attacks.

Among the prior inflammatory influences may properly be classed nudity, as at bathing beaches or burlesque shows—along with comic books, lewd pictures and books, and sexy movies. Yet such stimuli may be getting too great a share of blame for rapes and other sex offenses. For they not only build up sexual energy; they also act as release for it. They drain it off through vicarious experience. They provide a partial substitute, as one adolescent put it, "for the skin you love to touch." This boy, delegate at a high school forum on sex education, remarked: "Movies roused my curiosity about sex when I was a kid—but later they kind of satisfied it." Another delegate told the gathering, "The pictures smoothed me up, taught me how to get a girl without knocking her on the head."

Quite possibly, by this logic, the erotic moving picture or comic book prevents a far greater number of sex offenses than it provokes.

With rape, at any rate, responsibility would seem to lie in a quite different area. What would we ourselves do, those of us who are male, coming on a tempting girl such as Manya, over pubic age, alone and half-clad, in a setting of perfect privacy? Her very glance is coquetry, her ripeness a challenge. But we do not lose our heads—for fear of consequences, such as parenthood or arrest. Or we may be satiated, or owe loyalties to another. Perhaps we are too preoccupied with the problems of adulthood even to notice the girl. We may be physically weak.

But if none of these deterrents happen to apply, the only thing standing between our own selves and rape would be the girl's consent—or conscience!

Conscience? A voice sometimes of fear—fear of God. It may also bespeak love, for God and man. But always it is acquired, a thing of learning. It is the expression of countless moral teachings, warnings, promptings and pressures—all the conditioning factors which pound the animal infant into a social creature. Ask any mother the pains it takes to teach a child to be a respecter of persons! The pains have been taken with us. So we do not rape after all —we have been conditioned against it.

It is our social teaching, then, our culture, which inoculates us against rape.

Conversely, behind every rape stands cultural failure —most marked where cultural cohesion is lacking, where cultural tensions and conflicts emerge. So in individual as well as joint-rape, as might be expected, the South leads all the rest. *Rapes of Negro girls by white boys are relatively highest in Southern rural areas—the very places where miscegenation is most loudly condemned.* And since economic differences, as well as those of race or national origin, have a separating effect on cultures, scions of rich families contribute materially to rape statistics by ravishing servant girls in their households. These young rapists are so culturally distant that they tend to regard the poor, uneducated and possibly foreign-born or Negro girl as another species, not entitled to respect of person or any other respect.

These attitudes the youngsters pick up from friends and parents—the latter sometimes going so far as to actually encourage sexual offense. This case, though an extreme one, illustrates the point:

Pale Henry, 15 years old, was arrested today for raping

a girl of like age. The complaint came from the girl's mother, an impoverished cleaning woman.

The charge against Henry has opened up an array of new charges. Henry hates his father who is wealthy, thrice-divorced and a woman-chaser. But Henry's father supplies his son with funds and backs up his absences from school, in return for Henry's bringing young girls to their eight-room apartment.

Henry has pleaded guilty to the charge. But it has backfired in all directions. His father now faces trial for impairing the morals of a minor. And two of his father's girl friends, both above 21, and both of whom dallied with Henry prior to the present offense, are being sought for trial on charges of statutory rape; namely, the rape of Henry.

Nobody knows how many servant girls or field workers are raped each year—for Dad's bankroll or influence usually can hush the matter. Or, as the La Guardia Committee for the Study of Sex Crimes put it: "Nobody knows how many low-income offenders get caught and convicted because they lack the affluence or influence of more fortunately circumstanced offenders."

For that matter the number of all rapes of or by juveniles is impossible to determine or even guess at. Only a comparative handful claims the attention of police, courts or gossip circles. Penalties in shame and unpleasantness are such as often to seal mouths of victims. Families hesitate to brand wives contaminated, sisters less desirable, daughters less marriageable. When a rapist successfully operated for eight months around a college campus in Tennessee recently to the tune of twenty adolescents and women, it was chiefly because many victims kept silent that he was able to escape detection so long. And police had reason to believe that he had raped twice that many, though girlish reticence kept them from proving it.

Incidentally, the La Guardia Committee's report, covering rapes and other sex crimes in New York City during the 1930-1939 period, remains almost the only statistically exhaustive official study of the subject. Although now dated, the figures debunked at the time several myths to the effect that most sex criminals are homeless vagrants, paroled criminals, Negroes or foreigners, or brutish ape-men. The study revealed:

1. Of 4854 convicted offenders, only 2 percent had lived in New York less than a year; only 39 were homeless.

2. Of 3295 offenders, 39 percent had records of prior arrests—whereas among felons generally the number with previous criminal records averages 65 percent.

3. Of all sex crimes coming to the attention of police, district attorneys and courts during the studied interval, 80 percent were committed by whites.

4. Native-born Americans committed 73 percent of New York City sex crimes, a high ratio in view of the large numbers of foreign-born residents.

5. Sex offenders in the period formed no set type, physically or mentally. "The majority seem self-conscious and shy, rather than aggressive; usually they are of average intelligence."

One might expect that the ill-favored, the crippled, the scarred—handicapped in obtaining feminine favors—would be among the juveniles most likely to rape. The author has been unable to find mathematical verification of this popular view. In the previously cited 87 cases from New York, New Jersey and Pennsylvania, no offenders were reported malformed. A study of one hundred other boys of 18 or younger detained for rape shows one with a clubfoot, two with hand malformations, one a deafmute. I.Q. figures available for 43 of the latter group show three boys who might be classified as idiots or morons, and 36 boys with intelligence from dull to low-average. This may indicate, however, only that it is the dumb ones who get themselves caught.

The La Guardia report expressed "grave concern" over the rise in sex crimes among youths of 16 to 20. *This group accounted for one-fourth of all sex offenses in the period studied.* Fortunately, the boy over pubic age rarely rapes the girl below it. The taking of pre-pubic girls seems to be the province of pre-pubic boys and of adult rapists. The latter are either too timid to attack older girls, or so warped psychologically as to be incapable of satisfying themselves except with children.

In either case, their crimes fall under the head of aberration. So do those of the rare juvenile who rapes out of psychotic inability to enjoy girls except under brutal conditions. This lad does not participate in joint-rapes. He infrequently rapes on the spur of the moment. On the contrary, his characteristic is not only that he plays a lone hand, but that he carefully plans the attack. This deliberate planning for rape is typical of the aberrational or pathological rapist.

If cure or prevention there is for his condition, it lies in the province of psychiatry.

Aberration—used here to denote sex abnormality considered criminal or delinquent—takes various forms other than psychotic urges to rape. But let it again be stressed that regardless of form, the aberrational syndrome signifies disease. Sometimes the disease is organic, a product of undeveloped sex organs or glands, as in certain types of homosexualism involving hormone irregularities. More often it is psychological, a warping from pressures without or within.

Any juvenile sex expression, if in frequency or placement patently exceeding the norm, tends to be regarded as and incur the penalties of delinquency. Yet the excessively sexed and under-sexed are equally diseased; both deserve treatment—or punishment, if the latter is what we wish to reserve for disease. Nevertheless, it is solely the excessive sex manifestation which gets its day in court or clinic—as if potency could hurt the race, and impotency not!

This is based on the surmise that the strong or public sex manifestation may harm or annoy others, or set an example considered bad. And so it may. But it can be extremely tricky and unreliable as a measure of culpable delinquency. The high school boy leaning on a woman in a crowded bus is arrested. What for? Is she arrested for leaning on him? Or wearing a low neckline? Or being so devastatingly curved that she should know better than to poke bust or posterior at a male?

No; the degree or form of sex behavior gives no reliable index of culpability. Consider a rash of homosexual relationships which recently broke out among girls at a Long Island high school, alarming local civic groups and provoking a local newspaper to remark: "When the homosexual problem reaches alarming proportions, the causes are not individual or internal; they are external." Ministers and rabbis in the community took the same view, holding for psychiatric treatment of the girls—but warning the local citizenry that essential fault must lie somewhere in their own culture. Parents would either have to improve the general "moral" tone and repair psychological weaknesses imparted to their daughters—or give the kids, as a local physician proposed, " . . . easier opportunity to bed with clean, virile boys—in which case there would be no more of this homosexual nonsense."

But a majority of prominent residents were shocked less by the girls embracing each other than by newspapers and clergymen trying to embrace truth. Their view was, simply, that the girls were offenders. Hush up the whole thing, and lock them up. Punish them. That will teach them better— and other girls will fear to follow in their footsteps. No need to look to one's self, one's society, for the predisposing fault.

Of course, in all delinquencies there are contributing social influences. But the issue here is culpability, guilt. If aberration is a matter of doing what in the aberrant more or less "comes naturally," guilt is not clear. It lies, if anywhere, not in perversion as such, but in the uses to which perversion may be put. Should it be deliberately exploited for purposes otherwise violating law or morals, it becomes as recognizably reprehensible, at least, as any other delinquency.

To illustrate, in New York and a number of other cities since the war, boys of under 15 are known to be soliciting in the streets as homosexual prostitutes.

These unfortunates probably drifted into homosexual practice through sex curiosity or seduction by men. But after developing homosexual technique, they begin to frequent bright-light districts, as notably, in New York, Forty-second Street between Seventh and Eighth Avenues. There they solicit through bold glances and esoteric signs, often lingering in toilets, cinema houses and outside bars in the area. More than one sensational magazine article has described parties at which these children are used. Sometimes they are fed liquor, to heighten clients' hilarity. A number learn to blackmail—seducing "respectable" elderly men, then threatening to talk unless hush-money is paid. Police find it extremely difficult to prove anything against them—combat them chiefly by sporadic drives against "loitering."

But where does the turpitude lie? Not in the initial missteps of the boys; nor in their homosexual necessities, if indeed they have them. But rather in the deliberate trading of homosexualism for money.

This is not to say they are more delinquent or more to be punished than other kinds of delinquents—merely that they indulge in behavior which is genuine delinquency in the sense of any prostitution. Society, by its standards of right and wrong, can logically consider them culpable—assuming, of course, that the boys know what they are doing and know that prostitution is "wrong." It can logically attempt to correct them as delinquents, if not as sex aberrants. Aberration itself remains chiefly a matter for the physician.

Not so with behavior of the *precocious* type—sex escapades considered legally, morally or physically premature. It is difficult to know just why morals and law hold juvenile sex criminal or "delinquent" merely on grounds of precocity. Where sex behavior develops prematurely as a result of unnatural cultivation rather than natural growth, proscription is more understandable. But guilt, if any, surely lies with cultivator rather than cultivated.

Often enough precocity can be thoughtlessly encouraged, indeed, stimulated into being, by elders inflaming youngsters through erotic pursuits of their own. Thus, two men and three women were convicted in the Bronx after pleading guilty to impairing the morals of minors and possession of indecent photographs. Police, raiding on a tip, found the women lewdly exposed and the men taking indecent photographs—with three children present in the apartment!

But this is only an extreme example of the erotic atmosphere which commonly may surround a child in the normal course of events. Such an atmosphere is taken for granted in crowded tenement areas and plantation hovels, where privacy is impossible, where children may share the same bed as parents.

Incest, rape and a precocious sex life are bound to spring from such soil.

Or the sexual precocity may be deliberately induced by degenerate elders, often in quite young children. This constitutes true rape in all but the missing element of force, which cunning replaces.

The cunning usually consists, in such cases, of tempting the child to an isolated place by offers of toys or candy. Even this was not necessary in the many instances on police and medical records of adults handling children's parts until desire is created; infants so treated cannot be expected to react normally thereafter in their sexual responses. The thing is that the sexually precocious, though perhaps under the necessity of being watched or isolated for treatment, should be cared for in a way to avoid the stigma of detention or "delinquency"—or society would be rubbing salt in a wound of its own creating.

Of course, any man is at the mercy of the child who, accidentally touched or in sheer mischief, yells, "Rape!" A 49-year-old war veteran and his wife, he the employe of a prominent radio station in Newark, hanged themselves, after he had pleaded guilty to molesting a girl of 8 in a movie theatre. "He is innocent of any charge against him," wrote his wife in the suicide note. Who knows what peculiar circumstance led this apparently reputable husband and father to the alleged crime? Did he take too many cocktails that night? Perhaps he mistook the girl's age in the darkness.

Certainly on the known facts no one can accuse her

of egging him on, but more than once the legal infant has
turned up whose proclivities for sexual play get herself and
others into trouble.

One St. Louis girl of 10 was known to strike up acquaintance with a garage mechanic, and visit him eleven times for
sexual purposes before deciding to complain to police. A
maniacal degenerate who killed an 8-year-old boy in a west-
ern amusement park, hiding the body in an unused swimming pool, claimed he had been meeting the boy for immoral purposes, and killed him only because of the boy's
teasing threats to expose him. The boy, who came from a
comfortable home, had been seen with the killer several
times by playmates.

All this must be said not in excuse for criminals or mani-
acs who get themselves involved with children, but in recognition of a fact: to wit, certain children, even at early ages,
incite elders to sex experience even as elders incite them.
But only among older children—children past pubic age—
are deliberate incitements undertaken with sufficient frequency to be admitted a widespread problem. Here we
come into the recognized delinquency pattern of the "wayward" girl.

Again, the report on any one case duplicates almost line-
for-line the reports on thousands:

. San Francisco police yesterday booked five men of various ages from 17 to 30 on statutory rape charges and
announced they were looking for eighteen or nineteen
others suspected of having relations with a 14-year-old
girl.

Detective Hawley Edward said the girl, who ran away
from her Oakland home a month ago, had been sharing a
furnished room with a man for the past two weeks. Police
are searching for him.

Detectives picked up the girl and questioned her, after
having observed the five suspects entering and leaving
the room at various times.

The girl's mother, a widow, saw her daughter in detention yesterday. When told the girl would probably be con-

fined as a juvenile de'inquent, the mother said: "That's good—maybe it will be better that way."

Are such girls really "delinquent"? Surely they are either pathologically nymphomaniac—or congenitally feeble-minded. In either case, the codes by which the rest of us live pass them by. One cannot say "no"—the other does not know when to say it. Neither can be expected to take care of herself. Yet in very few places is help forthcoming for such children. In most states, after stopping for increasingly longer periods at "homes for wayward girls," they wind up in reform school, then in the reformatory, thus completing a course in how to become a prostitute, a thief or something worse.

Most boys and girls, when they precociously engage in sex relations, are being far more normal than abnormal. Further, they are sufficiently beyond feeble-mindedness to exercise a modicum of discretion. Only when the discretion breaks down do their names make the newspapers as "delinquents."

Here is a report from a beach resort not far from Washington, D. C.:

Authorities began a crackdown today on teen-age drunkenness, vulgarity and looseness among unchaperoned high school girls and boys vacationing at this Potomac River resort.

Most of the offenders are sorority and fraternity kids from Washington, D. C.

Six youngsters from Washington and Arlington, Va., were arrested on disorderly conduct charges in a predawn roundup, and fined $10 apiece. Mayor Norman F. Brewington said arrests would continue.

The offenses involve nudity, rape, drunkenness, rowdyism and all-night petting parties in cottages, automobiles and on the beach.

Loudness rather than lewdness brought down the authorities by giving the show away. Thirty days previously, public attention had been directed to similar revels by an unfortunate happening near Buffalo, N. Y.:

> The Long Beach (Ontario) Property Association has made an appeal to Buffalo and suburban parents and teachers to chaperone their children when they slip across the border to spend the night or longer at fraternity and sorority cottages.
>
> It is charged that the Buffalo high school students throw "wild parties" in the cottages, marked by nudity, "immoral behavior" and sex indulgence.
>
> The charges follow a fight at a beach party during which an 18-year-old Buffalo high school boy was shot and killed on the Canadian side of Lake Erie.

Drunkenness, rowdyism, shootings: these are overtly delinquent, to put it mildly. In these cases, they directed attention to sex situations duplicated among high school and other juveniles in many American areas. But for the most part sex relations, even at parties, are indulged in without breaking the peace. Without accompanying misbehaviors, it is difficult to put a finger on just where the delinquency lies.

This gives a peculiar quality to most sex "delinquencies." They are not antisocial in essence. It would be hard to prove that they harmed individual or racial survival. They do not molest, deprive no one of tangible goods. They may do psychological damage, but also psychological good; for they are as much acts of giving as of taking. Further, sex is no less natural than eating or sleeping, and, in the opinion of many juveniles, a lot more pleasant.

If allowed to satisfy appetites in one department, why the starvation in another?

Perhaps the socially dangerous aspect of juvenile sex, after all, lies not in its precocity, but in the fact that it achieves bliss without beatitude. It lacks the sanctification of marriage. Such a view has much in its support. Monogamous society's historical development bases partly on the idea that primarily sex is not for pleasure, but for child-begetting. Wedlock recognizes that economic responsibility must go with sex, for the sake of mother and child.

Contraception has interfered with the concept, whether we approve or not. So has the springing up of a general moral tone which, in this as in many past ages, assumes sex to be as much a pleasure-giving and soul-satisfying mechanism as one for impregnation. Even where contraception fails or is unknown, certain national or class groups accept economic support of mother and child, without marriage, as enough. This seems a mistaken view. It tends to deprive both mother and child of companionship, of the strengths and advantages of family life, of the atmosphere of love and close alliance which are among the chief social rewards of marriage.

9

Hayloft and High School

IN BOTH POPULAR AND JUDICIAL VIEW, THE YOUNGER adolescent is not mature enough for the responsibilities of marriage. But he may be quite mature enough for sex. Why should he oblige himself to wait? Practical considerations, as we have seen, are debatable, at least from the standpoint of the youngster. Moral tenets must prevail, then. He must control himself because it is "wrong" not to do so.

But such precepts coming from society must have some basis in the experience of man, some practicality of their own, or they are too metaphysical to affect children except through fear of punishment or the habit of obedience. Only the timid or meek would heed them.

Perhaps the whole idea of pre-marital sex as delinquent sex began in religious or moral intent to instil self-discipline and thereby make better human beings—like fasting on Fridays. Or it may link with some theme of denying present satisfactions for the sake of greater future ones. This is not the place to weigh the merits of such recommendations, which come backed by the accumulated experience of society. The point is that while holding the adolescent immature, they demand of him behavior representing the height of maturity! The infant cannot wait. The child is learning to do so. It is only the person adult indeed who can by will postpone today's physical pleasures for the spiritual ones of tomorrow.

So, unless its rewards are supremely convincing and well understood, many juveniles can only look on sex proscription as a punishment for being human. Puzzlement attends it, and resentment. Such a background in the child makes it easy for biologic compulsion to overwhelm social compunction—particularly when an adult assists the process.

And a willing adult can always be found, in open country as well as crowded city. Children who might hesitate to trust themselves to their own generation have been known to throw themselves at elders in whom they have confidence, and some elders have been known not to turn their backs. Cases of this sort are not so infrequent as might be supposed:

In an Oklahoma hamlet parents recently complained to state police that four young girls had vanished: Nora, 14; Lupe, 15; and a pair of black-haired, gray-eyed sisters, Gloria and Victoria, 13 and 11 respectively. Thirty-six hours before, Nora had had a date with Luke, a "stubby" 39-year-old farmhand who drove an old Chevrolet. Questioned, Luke readily admitted having taken the girls for a ride. He said they all had gone for a swim in Rock Pond, a few miles away, but they had refused to ride home with him, and he hadn't seen them since. "We had no bathing suits," he volunteered, "so we swam in our underwear." A few hours later, Nora, Lupe and one of the sisters were picked up 90 miles south on the highway, trying to thumb a ride in the direction of Amarillo, Texas. The other sister, Gloria, is still missing.

The story was played up by local newspapers, which considered the swimming episode good copy. They never got the more pertinent facts:

Gloria, the 13-year-old sister, was later found lurking near the fruit ranch which employed Luke. She had been extremely jealous of Nora, whom Luke would sometimes take to the movies at the county seat. She confessed that she had invited herself on the ride along with her sister and Lupe, a friend, in order to push her attentions on Luke. They had stopped for cokes at a service station on their way to the movies, and Gloria had suggested they drink them on the shore of Rock Pond. There she made advances to Luke, which he did not reject, but Nora interfered. Gloria then suggested a swim to the others, and giggling, they went into the water in the nude. They played and splashed with Luke until finally she induced him to take her on shore where they had relations. To placate Nora, Luke then had relations with her. Meanwhile, the 11-year-old Victoria, aping her sister, was trying to tempt Luke. After another swim, he satisfied her. Luke wanted to drive the girls back to town, but they decided to hitchhike to Amarillo, where Lupe had a cousin. Apparently they were ashamed to go back to town after what had occurred. Gloria, however, left them a few miles farther on and started back.

No psychometric or background information on the girls is available, but in the opinion of the sheriff none was particularly unintelligent. "Weren't bad girls either. Just full of pepper," a deputy stated in court. All were dismissed with warnings, including Luke.

In another case of orgy, this one from an old east coast community of less than a thousand population, the adult central figure did not find children throwing themselves at him, perhaps because he was close to 65 years old. He succeeded in winning their interest, and at the same time locating likely prospects, by opening the facilities of his home to adolescents in search of revelry. The account quoted is from a county newspaper:

A circle of kids from eighth, ninth and tenth grades in the consolidated school have been holding sexual orgies in the ramshackle farm near here of one of our best known citizens. Arraigned last night on morals charges involving children, he was held for the grand jury after admitting paying two local girls from 50 cents to 2 dollars for "small favors."

The girls, 13 and 12 years old, gave police information implicating at least eight other boys and girls in revels at the weatherbeaten farm. The 13-year-old says she was first brought to the house by a boy classmate. After several visits with the boy, she was approached by the accused, and admitted being intimate with him for 2 dollars. The 12-year-old stated, according to police, that she went there with other kids who were "making hay" on their own. She said:

"A lot of us kids used to go see him—he would give me a dollar and sometimes 50 cents and make me promise not to tell anyone about what he did to me."

The first break in the case came when the mother of the 12-year-old grew suspicious because her daughter began to stay out late, and was getting spending money from sources the child refused to reveal. The mother complained to township police—whose headquarters are only a stone's throw from the farm of the accused. Divorced a few years ago, he is over 64 years old and has two grown sons.

It will be noticed that both the cited cases—like the precocious sex incidents in the preceding chapter—were given away by contributing delinquencies; runaway brought official notice in one instance, prostitution in the other.

It will be noticed also that both cases took place in rural districts. This may be the place to bring up the whole subject of rural delinquency—child crime in small towns, villages and on the farm, as opposed to that in urban communities.

Rural delinquency constitutes a major class in any breakdown of juvenile crime types. Examining it here will be no digression since in a measure this will help our probe of sex as prenuptial delinquency. For in city districts large segments of the population look on intercourse prior to, or outside of, the marriage relationship with tolerance; so juvenile sex is regarded chiefly as a problem of precocity. But in agricultural sections the nubility of boys and girls at a much earlier age is taken for granted. Sex without marriage, rather than early sex, tends to be regarded as the issue.

By F.B.I. figures, rural crime as a whole was increasing at a rate at least three to four times as fast as city crime during the 1947-1948 interval. Continuing in the first six months of 1949, the rising trend included crimes of juveniles, and in 1948 showed a 4.6 percent increase in major crime categories over 1947, itself a year of increase. It would be a gross mistake to look on delinquency as primarily a city problem, a product of population concentration. It must be remembered that while rural schools spend only 70 percent as much per pupil as do city schools, almost one-half of all children of school age attend rural classes. A report by the U. S. Office of Education in 1945 analyzing the last interval of full survey, 1941-1942, showed more than 11,000,000 juveniles at that time going to schools in communities of less than 10,000; the number would be still greater today.

And among this great mass of kids every form of delinquency is encountered.

True, urban conditions sometimes breed, sometimes permit, certain characteristically frequent delinquencies, such as shoplifting. However, the farm has its own favored types; runaways and truancies, to name but two. And small towns may produce delinquencies considered quite exclusively big-city stuff, like gangsterism. We quote a statement to the press by Ed W. Thomas, Superintendent of Lackawanna Railroad Police—

We had a gang of Pennsylvania high school kids from Nanticoke and Glen Lyon. They were real hell raisers, all armed and vicious as they come. Before we finally caught up with them, they had committed 104 burglaries, 100 or so stickups, and stolen 157 cars! They smashed yard safes with sledge hammers and ransacked ticket offices; and when we got them they had a truckload of rifles and hardware.

They were caught when one of their stolen cars tipped over and we got the driver's license. A little tracing brought in the whole gang. Funny thing. They were tough and defiant when brought in; but after they started to talk all the bravado went right out of them and they became as meek as kittens. . . .

Shakedowns, maraudings, assaults, all the various iniquities of the city, are encountered in the country. And country boys show every bit as much ingenuity in getting themselves into trouble as do city juniors. In another Pennsylvania incident, near Lancaster, one 15-year-old went to the length of opening a kind of speakeasy in a secluded spot. Parents noted that children were walking around quite intoxicated, so that an investigation was launched by a special agent of the Pennsylvania Liquor Control Board. His researches led him finally to the "Kinderhook Athletic Association"—a shack near the culprit's farm home, where he was busily selling stolen beer and whiskey to some twenty children from neighboring farms!

But the one great conditioning element almost universal to rural delinquencies is sheer boredom; monotony unrelieved by the staccato excitements of city life, discontent with unpunctuated day-to-day routines. And the boredom may tend to relieve itself in sex.

Boredom lays a tinder for delinquency among city boys too. Youthful energy must be directed; youthful interest guided and aroused. Unless stimulation is forthcoming from those around him, only the exceptionally imaginative or ingenious child develops the interests to keep him from ennui. Here parent and school responsibility are at their highest; and in rural areas most often fail. Boredom, along with lack of local economic opportunity, drives large numbers of rural boys from the homestead. Some head for the cities where, they are told, the big, fast, exciting things happen. Others, following the only calling they know, become migrant workers.

The problem of these youthful transients has reached national proportions, evoking study in states throughout the midwestern farm belt, in Florida, in the Columbia River valley and the Southwest. The director of one such study for California, Mary B. Perry, Superintendent of Ventura School for Girls, declares of the adolescents she has investigated:

"They were not bums . . . but the kind of pioneering young people responsible for building the West. They should be encouraged and assisted in making adjustments in

California rather than be sent back to their legal homes without an analysis of their problems."

She points out that even in towns where housing and care are available to other transient youths, minority group youngsters find it "almost impossible to get any help outside of jails." In truth, in most states only the skimpiest and most scattered services of the kind, if any at all, are available for kids electing to seek work in rural areas. Under such conditions, it is less amazing that some get into trouble than that so many manage to stay out!

The migrant picture, as everyone knows, is complicated by whole families of farm workers who endlessly travel— *Grapes of Wrath* style—after the fruit and vegetable and sometimes the cereal harvests. Literally, they range from Maine's potato acres to California's truck farms, taking their kids with them. Says the National Commission on Children and Youth:

"Our states and communities have not yet built a system of assuring these migrant families the protection and services available to permanent members of the community. Frequently, mothers have little care at time of childbirth, children have no health services, little schooling, no access to recreation . . . and families are housed in unsanitary shacks and camps, often without adequate protection from the weather."

Some improvement has been observed since the end of the war, notably in New Jersey, Florida, California and a few other states. But essentially the child of a migrant family finds himself in a climate lushly productive of delinquency. Low living standards, low cultural levels, hard labor, pernicious monotony, housing conditions matching those of any city slum, these make it no wonder that behavior problems—including juvenile sex problems—breed prolifically!

Apart from the migrant, the rural boy in general tends to find his foremost delinquency outlet in sex. But he may develop other diversions much more easily that the rural girl, who even more than the boy finds herself locked in a routine, endlessly bored and proscribed on every side. Poor

girl! Even if she courts delinquency, almost the only way
open is through sex! As one "wayward" child told a Children's Bureau interviewer, "There ain't nothin' to do—and
what there is, ain't decent."

Thus we arrive again at the question of prenuptial juvenile sex adventure as a delinquency.

Some children run away and find sex in response to
blandishment, in the manner immemorial of maidens taken
in by traveling men:

A romance involving a 14-year-old East Keane girl and
a traveling carnival official led to an indictment today, in
which he faces Federal charges of transporting the child
from Vermont to Columbiana, Ala. for immoral purposes.

Named in the indictment is the 47-year-old concession
manager of the carnival. It is alleged that he induced the
girl to run away last summer to take a job in the carnival.

As often, perhaps, a girl desperate to get away deliberately traps the unwary:

Wilhelmina appears a wholesome, healthy girl, with a
milky complexion and a ready laugh. She talks with a
lisp. Complains that her father "makes fun of me." At
15, she ran away with 18-year-old Jacob. They lived in
rooming-houses and cheap hotels, all paid for by Jacob.

Recently she gave herself up and reported him, claiming he had made her run away. Her father supported the
story. Later facts showed she told Jacob her family beat
her and made her miserable, and had induced him to take
her away by playing on his sympathies. After two months,
he learned she was entertaining other men during his absences, and left her. She then complained to police.

Would marriage have aided either of these unions? Fun-
damentally, perhaps not, but no one can be sure. Possibly
the 47-year-old man and the 14-year-old maid were in deep-

est love, would have cherished each other to the end. Perhaps the marriage tie and more patience would have enabled gullible Jacob to correct the straying Wilhelmina. Yet these are remote possibilities. Both couples seem to have lacked the requisites for sustained and happy partnership. Either marriage, if accomplished, would almost certainly have ended as disastrously as it had begun. Only this would have been achieved: the "good name" of each girl would have been preserved.

But is reputation worth the sacrifice? Too often juveniles see that in their own circles the "bad" girls get the attention, the excitement—and at the same time the deep sensual pleasure of sex. What might seem to the girl a perfectly justifiable course would be the very one which could end in such tragedies as this, from South Carolina:

Jeannette was 15 years old last July. Blue-eyed, red-haired, weight 135, height 5' 6". Extremely attractive. Was a drum majorette at a consolidated school. Her father is an influential county resident.

Raymond, 23, admits having a date with Jeannette to drive to an isolated mountain cabin near Barok, 14 miles north in Cook County. They were to double date with Gary, 24, and Lou Betty, 16, girl friend of Jeannette, said to be very popular with men. The older girl failed to keep appointment due to illness, but Jeannette was "willing to go to cabin without a second girl." Both boys under questioning, admitted sexual relations with Jeannette at the cabin.

A souvenir 8-millimeter Japanese semi-automatic lay on the table. Jeannette had been "dancing and drinking pop" and was standing ready to leave. One of the boys picked up the gun and clicked the trigger once or twice. It clicked again and the gun went off, grazing the other boy's hand, and wounding Jeannette.

"I picked her up and ran toward the car. I knew Jeannette was dying. I was with her on the back seat and her head was on my lap. We were passing John's Ferry, almost at the hospital, when I knew she was dead. I never

dreamed the gun was loaded, I didn't think you could get
ammunition for a gun like that." So deposed the stricken
boy.

The father identified the body and swore warrants.
Both boys ex-Marines. A theory that the shooting occurred in a fight over Jeannette is being investigated.

If the accustomed thing in part of a group, sex indulgence is as communicable to the rest as the measles. Moreover, sex to the affection-hungry promises a way to comfort
and companionship. Add these pressures to isolation where
sex preoccupation prevails for sheer lack of any other, as
on a desert island or farm, and even the most stubborn girl
may fall. Examine these events of last winter, near Black-
foot, Idaho:

Imprisoned for three weeks in a snowbound farm during the recent blizzards, three couples revealed in court
today how they had whiled away tedium by swapping
partners nightly. The participants included Thornby, 32,
farmer; his wife Caroline, 30; Harry, 25, a friend; and
two girls—18-year-old Lucy and a 16-year-old whose
name was withheld. Also present was farm laborer
Nathan, who had happened to drop in just before the
snow.

Lucy and the younger girl had been sent some months
ago to help and board at the farm.

Thornby showed the court photographs of his pretty-
faced but 180-pound wife in a bedroom with Harry, saying that he had taken the pictures as a gag. All happened
to be in the house on February 4 when a blizzard hit the
crossroads with such fury that it was more than three
weeks before snowplows could get through. Details of how
the swapping started were hazy, but all seemed pleased
by their solution of what to do on snowy nights in Idaho,
until brought into court.

The district court judge sentenced the wife, Caroline,
and Harry to one year each. Nathan and the two girls
were recommended for probation. Thornby was sentenced

to three years, however, whereupon Lucy leaped to her feet and cried: "He shouldn't be sentenced to three years. If he is, then everyone deserves the same." She burst into tears and added, "He was forced into it!"

The court did not permit her to explain.

Details of the interlude first came to light some weeks after the big snow, when the 16-year-old girl suffered a nervous breakdown and was placed in a state home.

Again the pattern emerges. Each sex delinquency won notice not as such, but because of some associated occurrence. The carnival girl incurred search as a runaway—Wilhelmina gave herself up to police—Jeannette's sex life came to light through accidental killing—the Idaho spree escaped investigation until after the 16-year-old broke down mentally. To what extent juveniles sexually indulge each other and their elders is anybody's guess. But the author will hazard that by far the great majority of child sex episodes never become violently noticeable enough to cause them to be counted

In country localities more than city ones, the act of sex tends to presuppose that the partners are ready for it. Since the step from grace, then, consists only of avoiding the marriage obligation, it can be repaired simply by fulfilling the latter—and often is, under pressure of parents or the local community. In remote districts this kind of "shotgun wedding" results in a surprising number of unions at early ages. Another effect is the frequency of unions between child brides as young as 11 or 12 and men not merely mature, but sometimes in their dotage—and, less often, between youths and older women. Resolving delinquency in this manner (except perhaps where pregnancy is involved) may not appeal to us, but there is no use being holier-than-thou about it. If the marriages fail to work out, divorce or death of the older partner is always a rescuing possibility. In any case, it keeps both partners within the pale. They avoid the stigma of "immorality" or "delinquency"—and, as might happen in the case of a young girl, the institutionalization which could only lead to worse things.

To "civilized" folk, though admitting that such marriage may serve a purpose, the idea fails to appeal for one important reason; it may deprive a child of the rights of childhood. But it must be remembered that the adolescent on a Kentucky plantation or in the Ozark mountains may not want play and school and lack of social responsibility—considering himself quite ready for adult life, including parenthood. And so he—or she—may well be, by the demands and standards of the particular community.

Many rural pregnancies among juveniles, particularly, are settled by marriage. In a good many states the law is such that if children are too young for legal marriage, they are probably too young for pregnancy. If the male participant is already married to someone else when pregnancy reveals itself, perhaps a substitute can be found willing to become the husband. But if the girl is of evil reputation or otherwise ineligible for marriage, solution of illegitimate pregnancy becomes difficult. In the eyes of all, she stands manifestly delinquent. The responsibilities of both maternity and paternity may then become exceptionally tangled, as in this instance from rural Indiana.

When Florence, 17, brought a paternity suit against Gaspar, 19, the defense attorney wanted to show that practically anyone could have been the father of her child. He called on ten youths, all farm boys like the defendant and all 21 or younger, who testified in court that they had had relations with Florence at about the time the baby was conceived.

"This is a terrible situation," said the Circuit Judge. "I'm not sure what to do!"

The paternity case was then dismissed, and all eleven lads were charged with contributing to the delinquency of a minor, since Florence had been 16 when the intimacies had begun. The testimony stated that it had been a "popular sport" to take her riding with a group of boys, then give her a choice of walking home or submitting to sexual relations.

At the second trial, rather than deny the previous testimony and incur perjury, the boys and their parents accepted the suggestion of the defense attorney to set up a trust fund for support of the infant.

The judge acceded to the idea, and $1,375 was deposited in the girl's name.

The deputy sheriff who headed investigation of the case said the incident was part of a rising wave of juvenile delinquency in the Ft. Wayne area. "We still are trying to trace this mess to marijuana in the village where these young people live." He described it as a close-knit farm community of about 500, mostly of French-Canadian extraction. "This was a hard lesson for everyone," the deputy said, "but every so often in every town delinquency gets out of hand. Then you have to crack down—hard—with an object lesson."

The girl, reached at her family's farm, said: "I'm going to stay right here and raise my baby to be a good boy."

This lass was lucky. Not because of the trust fund. But because she had had a home during gestation, and now would have one in which to raise the child.

On the farm and in the city, when for one reason or another a girl becomes pregnant outside of marriage, she needs help badly. Often she gets it, from family, friends or the illicit father. But many girls must suffer through alone. At present rates, a minimum of 100,000 illegitimate births occur annually. The maximum is another of those "guess" figures so prevalent in estimates of delinquency, particularly sex delinquency. Some authorities state that for each recorded illegitimacy, another goes unrecorded. This would bring the annual total to somewhere near 200,000. But the producers of a recent Hollywood movie on the subject claim that a tour of public and private homes for unwed mothers in California turned up figures which, by extension, would mean a national total of 200,000 cases annually—among girls of 11 to 18 alone!

Unfortunately for accuracy—though fortunately for the babies who thus avoid stigma!—only 34 states keep records of illegitimacy. This explains much of the confusion in figures. But in 1946, the last fully surveyed year, these states showed 95,393 such births. And approximately half the mothers were adolescents.

It would seem, then, that at least two or three of every hundred babies are illegitimate, and that at least 40,000 to 50,000 "juveniles" become unwed mothers each year.

What happens to these mothers of children, who are really children themselves?

Prenuptial sex being generally considered immoral, and this view being reflected in statutes which make it illegal, let us grant that the unwed teen-age mother is a delinquent.

But the crime is not so great that society may not consider her shame and pain sufficient price for the delinquent act. Also, the act is of a nature to make its own restitution. The sinner brings society a gift. For the sake of its own health, society may wish to accept this gift and give the child as good a start as possible. It may wish to guard the mother against further difficulties, her trouble meaning trouble to itself. Or it may simply wish to serve her and the child out of humaneness.

So a split has appeared in society's machinery. In most states, statutes arbitrarily classifying the mother as a delinquent remain on the books—but private and public welfare facilities hope nobody puts in a complaint against the young lady; *they* certainly won't.

Thus, in New York City, a paradoxical situation exists. If parents put in a complaint against a pregnant daughter, the Girl's Term in Magistrates' Court and other judicial divisions dealing with teen-agers must arbitrarily sentence her. The girl is sent away to Westfield State Farm or the correction home of the Sisters of the Good Shepherd. She is allowed one month at a hospital to bear the baby, then is sent back to the institution to finish her sentence. The baby may be returned to her if the institution has facilities for it, or it may spend its first, formative months away from its mother in such places as the New York Foundling Hospital.

If only the parents would not complain—and often the

judges beg them not to—the erring girls would escape spending the pregnancy period surrounded by purse-snatchers, prostitutes, psychopathic degenerates. Says Chief Magistrate Bromberger: "Such girls may be tenderly cared for at home, or through home efforts and facilities processed through public agencies such as the Welfare and Hospital Departments."

In New York, should the unwed mother avoid being sent away as a wayward minor on somebody's complaint, she can get excellent help from several agencies. The Welfare Department, for example, will not preach or ask questions, will assist with financial and medical aid, and if called upon to do so may even supply legal assistance in suing the father for support. Similar services are available in Chicago, Los Angeles and a number of other cities. But the same divided approach often prevails, some girls being well cared for—others winding up in reform homes and institutions as sexual delinquents.

The split, of course, reflects a cleavage of opinion throughout the population. In a rural area, the girl may have a better chance to get the support she needs at home, perhaps because rural families are closer knit and require more to knock them apart—or it may be just that welfare facilities are not as available as in the cities. But many a rural child-mother finds herself obliged by stern attitudes to leave home, whereupon she probably heads for a city to swell the ranks of girls requiring assistance. In some communities, she can get it. Others refuse it on the ground that she is a non-resident. In many she is considered strictly a delinquent, eligible for help only through banishment to an institution. And in all cities, whether or not they wish to treat her generously, facilities are likely to be woefully short. In the whole United States, there are not more than 225 listed pregnancy homes to which an unwed mother can voluntarily gain admittance. These can accommodate more than 30,000 annually, but this figure includes adult as well as adolescent mothers, the latter often finding themselves crowded out.

As an alternative more attractive than suicide, a certain

number are driven into so called "black market hospitals" which derive a profit from supplying babies for adoption in return for a fee. At these illegal, unsanitary dives, the pregnant girl works in return for her keep, has her baby at the hands of inept, unqualified practitioners. The infant is then taken from her, a birth certificate forged, and the mother driven into the street. The remaining choice is abortion—except that most girls have scruples against it or can't afford it.

The situation does not reflect credit upon us. Statistically, unwed mothers represent a cross section of the population. As a group they show no special drawbacks in intelligence or other inferiority as human material. Often enough it is the relatively innocent girl who gets into trouble, rather than "bad" ones who know about contraceptives and abortions.

And the unwed mother's crime, if any, is against herself and her baby; she has the same social right to be defended from crime as any of us. Justice, if not mercy, indicates that she be provided the help she needs.

Some 5 to 7 per cent of all delinquencies acted on in juvenile courts are listed as sex delinquencies. Various rapes and allied types of assault are listed in the "injury to person" category rather than as sex offenses. Sex indecencies, by their nature, are often prevented from reaching court by folks moving heaven and earth to keep them private. Further, it is the girls who tend to get themselves arrested for sex indulgence; even the law and its officers seem to pursue a kind of double standard, arresting a girl for promiscuity —but not the boys who have been partners to it. Thus, in 1944, 3 percent of all boys disposed of in juvenile courts were reported as sex offenders, and 18 percent of girls. In 1945, the percentages ran exactly the same. Later breakdowns are not complete, but it would appear that if participant boys were hauled into court along with their girl friends, the number of sex offenders would reveal itself as much higher. From this, the author feels safe in estimating that sex offenses comprise a good 8 to 10 percent of all delinquencies.

But that does not complete the statistical story. Sex offenses are highly private crimes. Robberies nearly always are reported, bringing reaction from police. Sex delinquencies, far more often than not, go completely unreported. Most, as we have seen, would never reach public notice at all were it not for some accompanying delinquency.

We may deduce, then, that sex delinquencies raise the total of delinquency, and comprise a part of that total, to a far greater extent than is at first apparent. The facts on unwed mothers, along with numerous though fragmentary figures compiled by various social agencies, courts, probation groups, the New York Academy of Medicine, and such individual researchers as Kinsey, would seem to bear this out. It also must be borne in mind that in rural areas, where sex offenses may be relatively most numerous, they most rarely reach court.

In brief, it may not be quite true, as one Chicago daily screamed in an alarmed banner, that: *MORALS BREAKDOWN THREATENS YOUTH OF COUNTRY*. But juvenile sex delinquency is far more prevalent than generally suspected.

Evidently, then, moral proscriptions and prohibitions are not achieving any startling success in stemming the sex proclivities of youngsters. Why?

Is it because the promises of later reward seem false, the game of waiting not worth the candle? Possibly.

But we have seen that sex delinquency, in case after case, occurred in association with other and usually more severe delinquencies or behavior problems. Promiscuous sex, precocious sex, sex without marriage, these tend to lead kids into other trouble. And illegitimate motherhood, despite every precaution, may ensue with all its train of sorrow. These, to a minor, may appear doubtful objections. Balance and personality-soundness might preclude a bit of sex from becoming a wedge for other delinquencies; motherhood generally can be avoided, often can be solved by marriage if worst comes to worst, may even prove a blessing to those with the heart for it. But the answer is difficult to a third consideration. Sex tends to place a juvenile, especially a girl, in a critical position in this way: *the crime may not seem real to the participants, but society considers it so—and may exact penalties*. Put another way, the morality of our time may not be correct, perhaps should be changed—perhaps is in process of change. Meanwhile, however, it remains the one we must live with. Breaking it means that we are not going along with society. So there may be certain practical advantages to continence, to a temperate sex approach, after all!

The trouble is, a lot of kids just don't believe it. Church, school, family, the voices of society, fail to convince.

Because from what they see, sex looseness would not isolate them from society; it would make them a part of it! Too many elders preach with word but not with action; the whole world around these children screams that its promises and recommendations are false—for otherwise adults would take them more seriously! Instead, they indulge in all kinds of sex irregularities, at home, in cars, at bars and nightclubs. They talk about sex indulgences themselves, put them on screen and stage and into books. Revered elder brothers returned from the wars are full of past sex experiences and looking forward to fresh ones. Newspapers are filled with lurid tales of sexual horseplay. The fact is that elders set up a code for youngsters, and themselves knock it down. Even if he comes from an excellent and well-mannered home, the growing adolescent can hardly avoid encountering evidences of widespread sexual promiscuity. Why should he heed preaching?

Can the situation be corrected through some other means, then?

Many recommend sex education, of which there is a woeful lack both at home and in schools. We may accept the necessity for such education as vital. It would render the juvenile happier; and certainly safer. Besides, he has a right to sex knowledge, as to any knowledge.

And unquestionably it would help turn the sex urge into healthier channels, avoiding incidents such as the following:

In an Atlanta, Ga., high school recently, teachers and classmates gradually accumulated evidence to show that a circle of boys had been behaving in a strange way. Inquiries met with embarrassed silence, but the teachers finally learned that 10 boys had formed themselves into a "cult" devoted to obscene practices among themselves. These included homosexual practices, mutual masturbation, investigation of obscene literature and the like.

All the boys came from good families in comfortable circumstances. But in juvenile court, Judge Garland Watkins heatedly criticized: "Not a single mother or father of these boys had given them any instruction whatsoever in matters of sex."

Possibly, also, sex education would forestall certain types of rapes and sex crimes in which innocents permit themselves to be led to slaughter: the child responding to an "affectionate" caress in a movie theater, the adolescent accepting a ride from a leering stranger. "If anybody had told me some men were peculiar," writes an anonymous teenager in a national journal, "I could have been saved the shock of finding it out from a peculiar man." But the same boy's discussion of sex education from the teenster's angle indicates how carefully it must be handled. "I don't know —I'm no psychologist—but maybe for kids starting out, rape and murder and sex should not be connected." He adds, "What one (educational) movie showed was venereal disease and how it worked on bodies. And a Caesarian operation. Some girls screamed and some had to go to the restroom."

Almost certainly, sex education could lower the venereal rate, and not by instilling fear and disgust, but rather by teaching prevention and cure. And we concur with those who believe it would diminish the incidence of unwed mothers—though the U. S. Children's Bureau itself does not wholly agree, feeling that the youngsters' "emotional wellbeing" at home would better "reduce the chances for unmarried mothers in their generation."

But as for cutting promiscuity and the extent of juvenile

indulgence—which so many advocates of sex education say it will—we feel this to be most doubtful.

Philosophical admonitions about "spiritual embodiment" and the beauties and advantages of postponement do not impress adolescents. At countless forums, discussions and meetings among teen-agers, they have tried to impress on the adult world that what they mean by sex education is practical education. "The facts of life," as the 1949 conference of "boy governors" in Washington, D. C. expressed it, "by teachers especially trained." The kids want plain talk —practical information, in order to make practical use of it. In the opinion of the author, sex education would be successful only if it completely removed areas of fear, doubt and ignorance; but these are the very things which keep millions of young folks out of each other's embraces!

So again we are thrown back to the conclusion that not sex education, but moral education, is the one great counterforce to physical urge. And this to a degree is failing because the adult, though preaching the lesson, fails to live it.

The most effective cure for sex delinquency, it follows, would be a change in the milieu, the general moral surroundings. But if adults remain unwilling to alter their sex manners, some relief from juvenile sex offenses might be afforded by:

1. Lessening of cultural tensions through teaching democratic respect for all individuals. This would especially help against certain types of rape.

2. Close attention to early behavior problems—particularly those indicating faulty inhibitory processes, low sexual thresholds, and boredom. This might rescue some children before they could seriously stray, and would have the advantage of isolating the pathological child before he became dangerous to others.

3. Building up control and temperance through proving the advantages of self-discipline in behavior areas other than sexual, where they may be easier to demonstrate. The rounded personality inclines toward moderation

10

Cradles of Crime

HAVING LOOKED AT VARIOUS TYPES OF DELINQUENTS
and kinds of delinquencies, we may now go more deeply into
questions of over-all remedy and prevention. Properly, attempts at remedy might be expected to begin virtually as
soon as a youngster's crime brings him into the hands of the
authorities. But what actually happens when a suspected
delinquent is arrested? How is he handled? Are immediate measures taken to set his feet in proper paths? Is he put
into surroundings conducive to correction?

Inspectors of the Federal Bureau of Prisons recently took
a look at 3000 state, county and municipal jails in our land.
As they were merely seeking accommodations for Federal
prisoners, the inspectors were not being too choosy. Yet
they had to report that some 2400 of the investigated jails
were unfit to hold adult offenders.

These are the very jails which lock up thousands of children each year!

Here are some of the inspectors' reports, quoted from gov-
ernment sources:

The X—— jail was . . . dirty . . . revolting . . . I
found one-fourth of the jail population made up of children under sixteen . . . scattered through the jail . . .
one had been brought in twenty days before by two railroad policemen. The boy's mother was dead, the father
was doing his best to keep the family together. The boy
was trying to do his part by salvaging bits of coal from
the railroad tracks . . .

*　　*　　*

In a city of almost a million . . . no proper place for

holding children. In jail that day were 72 children, sixteen or younger. They sleep in same cells with adults, eat in same dining room, associate with them during dragging hours of the day.

* * *

. . . Boys and girls crowded into cells. Unusually large number of children in this jail in a county where there was a juvenile court. Since first part of June, boys and girls had been held, waiting for the juvenile court which did not convene until end of August. All through the summer for 24 hours a day these children had been in jail in small cells. Most serious charge I could find . . . stealing a few packages of cigarettes. Some not more than twelve years of age. For petty thefts where a man might be given 30 days, they had already served three months without a hearing.

Another survey yielded the following comment, also from Federal sources:

In a certain city without juvenile detention facilities, the jails and county prison farms were used for the purpose. A probation officer in this city recently received an inquiry from the welfare department of another state, saying, "A runaway girl has just been returned to our custody by you. Her report of her stay in your county prison farm alarms us. We realize that she may have made up the whole story, but for your own information and protection you might want to investigate." The escaped girl's tale told of terrific overcrowding of women prisoners, complete lack of privacy and sanitary protection, rampant homosexual attacks, bad food, filth, vermin, idleness, craven and bestial behavior.

The probation officer smiled at the apologetic tone of the inquiry, and made this reply: "I don't need to investigate. It's everything she said—and worse!"

Remember, most children in such jails are merely being

"detained." *In a good proportion of cases, not a thing has been proved against them!* They are simply being held on charges, awaiting trial.

In many other cases, the youngster has had his day in court, but is awaiting—with what inner tensions, heaven only knows—his sentence or disposition. The "detention" stage is merely a stop-over on the way to reformatory, training camp, welfare agency—or, for the lucky ones, probation in their own homes.

Only a small portion of our youth in jail is supposed to be actually serving sentence there. According to Federal Advisory Panel information in 1946, every state in the union boasts at least one institution for "reforming" or "training" delinquents. It is to such places all "detained" juveniles are supposed to be transferred.

Yet we know this same panel estimates that perhaps 300,000 kids under eighteen are "detained" each year, in jails or temporary "detention homes." And Russell Sage Foundation figures indicate that the combined population of all state, county, municipal and semi-official though privately operated "reform" schools, reaches some 30,000 to 40,000.

What happens to the other 260,000 youngsters in trouble?

Do they engineer successful jail breaks and disappear? Even allowing for the thousands declared innocent, returned home on probation or suspended sentence, or remanded in custody of relatives, foster homes and private groups, one thing remains clear. Other thousands, each year, whether or not they make the statistics, never reach the special schools supposed to rehabilitate them.

Simply, they serve out their sentences in detention homes —or assorted jugs, calabooses and jails!

Most of which are found, even by hardened Federal prison inspectors, to be utterly unfit for human habitation!

At least 10,000 police jails alone were counted in America by Hastings L. Hart, the penologist, as far back as 1932.

A recent coordinated effort by Federal, state, municipal and private agencies—with the support of the President of the United States and the specific sponsorship of the Attorney General—failed to determine just how many children languish in such jails. In 1946, the National Probation Association compiled various inmate figures, including those of certain of the best juvenile detention facilities in the country. According to the rate at eleven of the latter, detention over the nation would be some 40,000 annually. But this represents a minimum guess, for communities with advanced facilities are not inclined to jail children at all. What the maximum possibility is no one has dared estimate—perhaps out of shame.

For this is the twentieth century! How are we, citizens of enlightened America, to excuse ourselves for jailing children at all?

Nine out of ten juvenile jailbirds are released or moved on within a month. But thirty days can be a long time for an acute disease to languish without treatment. The disease not only goes uncured; it is deliberately aggravated. Kids can learn a lot in a few days . . . that all society is against them, for instance, classing them with assorted burglars, forgers, perverts and thugs.

At the very time the youngster most needs parental guidance or its equivalent—family-type conditions—mental and physical hygiene—a feeling that somebody is on his side—the very things, in short, whose lack made him a delinquent in the first place, what is he given? Locks and bars. A turnkey for guide and counselor. An assortment of bums and criminals for brothers.

Read this parole officer's report about a girl in Texas:

Maria, aged 15, Mexican parentage, was picked up in five-and-ten cent store with a group accused of stealing jewelry.

She denies guilt; admits having entered the store with other girls. High-spirited, strapping build, at least average intelligence, English somewhat broken.

Maria's offense, plus continued school truancy, plus sullen, angry behavior in court, plus violent attempts to resist arrest including injuring police officer by throwing hammer seized from counter, brought her a 60- to 120-day sentence, supposed to be served out in L—— training school, too overcrowded to accept her. While awaiting vacancy, she is completing sentence in police jail.

This jail is also crowded, so she shares cell with two other delinquents. First, age 17, is being held on prostitution charges. Second, age 19, is a third-time repeater, awaiting sentence on prostitution charges. Latter venereal. Adjoining cell holds larceny prisoner, age 54, awaiting transfer to psychopathic prison ward. Other adjoining cell populated by procession of prostitutes, alcoholics etc.

Maria is angry over sentence, appears to believe in own innocence. During the first week she bitterly refused cooperation; was put in solitary, 36 hours, for crying and outbursts bothering other prisoners. She emerged from solitary apparently bent on revenge, attacked prison matron from behind. Put back in solitary, 48 hours. On release, she awaited chance, attacked food attendant with shoe. Cellmates, amused, egged her on. Given bad beating by attendants.

After this, Maria subsided somewhat but remains easily aroused. Knowing this, inmates tease her, calling her "greaser," "crook," "whore" etc. Disciplined several times for violent fights with inmates. Matron and attendants also seem to take pleasure in provoking her to spitfire tantrums, then punishing her for same. Claims matron brought in two police officers late one night from police headquarters (on floor below in same building). Claims matron then entered cell and deliberately aroused her to fury by name-calling, pinching, ridiculous orders, etc. Claims police officers, laughing, then disciplined her, one laying her across his knees while the other spanked her, and also struck her several times with his belt. Cellmates and matron deny this incident, but girl exhibited bruised arms, buttocks and back. Feels desperate and friendless. *60-day report:* Parole recommended to remove girl from present surroundings.

Parole was denied, on the ground that there existed no evidence of good behavior. The author attempted to follow up Maria's case some six months later, curious as to the after-effects of her stay behind bars. The parole officer had no further information, nor had the court originally responsible for sentence. No agency in town did follow-up work with released juvenile offenders. Police officials would not show even the original records. They were quite righteous about it. The girl had evened her debt to society, said they, and now was entitled to be left alone.

In view of the obvious drawbacks, should not all jailing of children be prohibited by law? Definitely—and in twenty-eight states, it is. But often "older" and "more difficult" children are excluded from the law's benefits. Or, as in the case of Maria, detention or rehabilitation facilities are so crammed that not another kid can be stuffed into them. In other words, children remain in jail because there is no other place for them to go.

This, too, is a common reason for child imprisonment in the remaining twenty states. Some of these require counties to operate juvenile detention centers apart from jails, but in the words of a Federal panel report, "this does not assure their establishment."

This report points out further that since some states pay local jails a daily sum for the "care and feeding" of inmates, abuses are inevitable. *In the United States—this very day—are children being detained simply to keep jails full and the expense money rolling in?*

But there is a far greater obstacle to clearing filthy, crime-breeding jails of scared kids. Too many of us, alas, still think that punishment is cure! This view remains popular even among numbers of police, penal and judicial officers—who should be the first to know better.

You may recall a statement widely quoted in the newspapers not long ago, coming from a judge in the Middle West: "48-hour solitary confinement in jail for every juvenile offender would do away with repeaters." His prescription was promptly endorsed by a die-hard element from coast to coast, including a prominent juvenile court justice in a large eastern city. Yet every statistic, every investigation, demonstrates that bars are bad medicine. While proper punishments, like proper pills, may have some place in a healing process—and even that much is doubtful—certainly confinement in any jail exerts an exactly wrong effect. For it does not reform, it deforms. It twists.

"This is no sob-sister sentimentality . . . *jailing a child will never frighten or shame him into reforming.* We now see that when society jails youthful offenders, instead of protecting itself from them it makes them the more determined, the more distrustful, the more cunning and resourceful in their enmity toward society." The italics are ours. The words are those of the Justice Department's National Conference on Prevention and Control of Juvenile Delinquency.

Other than jails, what are American detention facilities like? These are not to be confused, you understand, with reform schools or training establishments. They are merely places where children are held away from home, temporarily, pending disposition.

And there are some good ones. Take "boarding home" detention. The best example, perhaps, is found in a New York State community of roughly a million population. Less than a dozen such homes—which are no more than boarding houses privately operated by qualified couples, and admitting delinquents exclusively—are able to handle all but one or two local cases a year. The latter are pathologically aggressive or mentally unstable, and are jailed or hospitalized for safety's sake. The boarding homes take in either boys or girls, never both, and two or three serve as receiving homes —accepting new boarders at any hour, night as well as day. These are later transferred to other homes, meanwhile having had the advantage of being spared a number of hours in police lockup or jail. The city pays the boarding home proprietors a fixed rate per inmate, and provides special teachers who spend a few hours weekly at each one.

This plan is in wide use in numerous communities, not always with as happy results.

Disadvantages? Lack of twenty-four hour supervision

A certain sparsity of activity, due to limitations of space and material, and flagging interest on the part of the boarding parents—who after all are only human. Also, such homes sometimes prove unsuccessful for offenders over sixteen years of age.

Advantages? Flexibility: Children can be grouped in the various homes by ages or other characteristics—and a child unhappy with one parent can be moved to the supervision of another. Home atmosphere, small groups, tend to quiet aggressive youngsters and take the glamour out of being "tough."

A second type of detention center is the "residence home." It resembles the boarding home almost exactly, but is owned or leased by the community. Every attempt, at least theoretically, is made to maintain homelike atmosphere. Operation is by a paid staff; a married couple, for instance, with assistants. This permits something closer to around-the-clock supervision than occurs in the boarding homes, but otherwise the advantages and disadvantages of the residence home are about the same. Residence-type detention is sometimes called the "Massachusetts Plan" because of its successful use by certain large communities in that state.

Widely relied on, rather than homes, are the detention "institutions." These vary from mere residence homes grown oversize to enormous barred barracks. They may be state-controlled and regional, as in Connecticut, or strictly local, as in New York City. One city of 750,000 successfully combines boarding homes with a small type of institution. Children under twelve, and older ones deemed suitable, go to homes. Tougher customers who can bear watching are detained in the institution. Nevertheless, the latter is without cells or bars, and skilled supervision has been able to preserve, if not a home atmosphere, at least a wholesome one.

If small enough, the well-conducted institution definitely can retain most of the good features of a home. The larger it grows, of course, the greater the pitfall of demoralizing side-effects. The chief danger lies in the distance between the

supervision at the top and the child at the bottom. The
child tends to become a number. Activities become mere
routines. Impersonalized supervision substitutes for intimate, homelike control possible in a small circle. Under
these circumstances, to again quote the Advisory Panel,
"conditions are ripe for delinquency contagion, for the
development of youth-against-the-world atmosphere, and
for spirals of aggression."

Just the same, experiments in several cities have shown
that careful splitting up into sharply separated units may
eliminate most of the evils of size. Each unit, complete with
living, dining and recreational equipment, lends itself to
close, personal supervision. Children may be distributed
among them according to age and other characteristics.
Even in the almost insuperable task of humanizing large
institutions, we see, intelligence and good will can work
wonders!

But to what degree, actually, are intelligence and good
will devoted to the detention problem? What share of attention, understanding—and public funds—are its portion?

In 1945, the National Probation Association began an investigation of detention places for minors. It left out the
jails. It was looking for a few institutions or homes which
were working well, so that the membership could get some
idea of how best to handle juvenile offenders.

The association consists not of professional do-gooders or
visionaries, but of practical people working around prisons
and prisoners. They did not expect too much. Knowing
that if investigators were ordered to visit only model facilities they would probably never even have an excuse to
leave town, the association was willing to settle for homes
with even one worthwhile feature. Seeking such places for
its investigators to investigate, it got shocking replies from
state welfare and correction bureaus.

Many, as we know, could report no detention facilities
save jails. Others had one or two detention homes, but ad-

mitted they rated visits only from slumming parties. Even where states required special detention facilities by law, *some could suggest not a single home boasting a single redeeming feature of the kind sought by the association!*

Nice, isn't it? The investigators felt discouraged, for which we can't blame them. But they were even more discouraged, later, after visiting the places recommended, if not as "best," then as "least worst"—sixty-eight of them, scattered over twenty-two states.

They reported two characteristic types of detention homes. In the first, "poor building, lack of segregation (by age and psychological need), under-staffing, lack of trained personnel, and low budget throw mixed groups of children unsupervised into bull pens and crime schools." In the second, a fine building is kept "as a showplace" with an untrained staff trying to serve "twice as many children as a trained staff could handle." The result? "A vicious system of regimentation at cross purposes with everything we know about making useful citizens out of erring youth."

What is it like inside these detention homes—which, remember, far from being the worst of their kind, rate among the best that the inspectors could turn up.

In the one kind, bare furnishings add to a pervading atmosphere of gloom. Since supervision consists of one or two matrons on the ground floor, locked doors and bars separate the girls on the second floor from the boys on the third. Meals and infrequent exercise jaunts provide some relief, but for the most part the separate sexes spend day and night completely cut off and unwatched behind their respective barred doors. This makes things bad for the younger children, including feeble-minded kids and occasional babies below nine, locked up indiscriminately with hardened delinquents of sixteen or seventeen.

Why is this classed among the "average or better" places? Well, it does separate children from adult convicts—it keep boys away from girls—and its locks are plentiful enough to discourage escapes. Yes, and quarters are kept dutifully scrubbed—even though they may be disintegrating from old age!

Now, let us sample the second type of home—the one with a "showplace" building.

This, indeed, is spacious and well-maintained. And here the lack of supervision characterizing the other home is not tolerated. The children, instead, are watched every second of the day and night! No individual activities are allowed, no individual possessions—even a hairpin. This happens to be a detention home for girls, from thirty to forty delinquents between the ages of 9 and 16. Are they allowed to roam around in idleness and worse behind locked—but at least fairly private—doors? Not on your life. Here they must be observed every minute and doing something every second—scrubbing, sweeping, dusting, or playing checkers and reading comic books in a guarded dayroom. This routine is interrupted several times a day by line-ups—to be counted, searched, or to use the toilets. There is an hourly play period in the courtyard each day, but no equipment or program. If one or two girls wander apart to talk or play, they are commanded to rejoin the group. Will all this make a girl want to live a better life, asks the Advisory Panel report. "Not a chance. It will tell her a hundred times a day that the adult world distrusts, despises, blames and hates her. She will distrust and hate right back."

The same report mentions another "fine looking detention home" with a well-furnished living room in its boys' quarters. The room is proudly shown to visitors, but the boys are allowed into it only four hours per week. The rest of the time they spend locked in a dayroom with bare benches for furniture—"alone without leadership or occupation." Adds the report delicately: "The attendant—who is no more than a keeper—depends on a uniform cap to increase his authority with the boys." In another city, the curious dean of a local college was looking around in a detention institution, and to her surprise unearthed a goodly cache of unused play equipment. "Why bother with it?" an official responded to her outraged query. "These kids are all headed for reform schools, aren't they?"

But at the same detention home, another kind of toy is popular enough—the paddle. A doctor's routine examination of a fourteen-year-old boy, removed for a court hearing, revealed bruises four inches in diameter. Of another home it is reported: "Within thirty minutes of admittance, a twelve-year-old had been beaten with a belt by older boys because he did not have any money or cigarettes."

In the below-average detention centers, abuses are far worse. It is no secret that solitary confinement, bread-and-water diets and beatings fall to the lot of hundreds of child-prisoners each day.

Is the detention picture hopeless, then? Not by any means. True enough, conditions have not changed much since the National Probation Association's survey in 1945. But a few pages back, we mentioned examples of various types of sound facilities in certain communities. And what one town can do, another can.

A few years ago a certain Michigan city boasted a detention home considered one of the worst in the country. Things got so bad that suddenly people just refused to stand for it. They threw out the administration—installed a new one with orders to improve things, or else. . . .

Today this very home, of the small "institution" type, ranks among the nation's best. The barred cages that once held children now store potatoes. Since skilled personnel proved hard to get, a training course was set up under staff supervision. Local churches and clubs kicked in with paint and decorating supplies—play and craft materials.

Again, in 1944 and 1945, with youthful delinquents so flooding its private boarding homes that conditions in them were scandalous, a goodly number of New York City residents yelled for action. They were not ashamed to make a noise. For while people dispute about practically everything under the sun, on one subject they all agree. Kids are swell —even if they do go off the beam once in a while.

Most New York detention quarters at that time were operated by the Society for the Prevention of Cruelty to Children. The society's nice title had been enough to reassure New Yorkers—until a newspaper series (by Evelyn

Seeley, of PM) raised a scandal. People were aroused to anger. Official investigations followed, confirming the Seeley charges. Public pressure became so strong that the city hastily set aside a building of its own to receive boys up to sixteen years of age from Manhattan, Bronx and Brooklyn.

Called *Youth House*, the building itself is a depressing affair, located on the lower east side. Its facilities are not exceptional. It looks forbidding and gloomy. It gets by on a relatively small budget, though it handles a floating population of up to 120 boys. At first matters were so confused that during the initial month of operation no less than 93 rascals broke out of the place!

But Youth House has the one most important asset in detention care: an enlightened staff. Personnel relies on friendliness, on trust. Punishment of any kind is banned. "These kids have been punished enough before they get here," believes the director, Frank J. Cohen. "Punishment is not a deterrent factor, whereas good will and understanding are. Delinquent boys want to be considered decent and upright, and respond enthusiastically when given trust and confidence." No child is treated with hostility, no matter what the provocation; instead, he is encouraged to talk about his problems, to get his complaints and bitterness off his chest. Children are divided into groups according to age and behavior characteristics, each group being assigned its own dormitory and play room. Friendly, encouraging supervisors are constantly on hand—but regimentation is conspicuous by its absence!

Under such administration, it took only a few months for Youth House to far outdistance most detention facilities in this country. Boys who pass through it, treated with neither cloying sentimentality nor grating harshness, go their separate ways certainly no worse off than they were before—and in most cases with new hope and courage, a feeling that a boy in trouble is not totally friendless in this world.

Nor does this kind of approach enjoy any less success with girls. The same hue and cry which caused the establishment of Youth House led Fiorello La Guardia, then mayor, to open an emergency detention center for girls on Welfare Island. This was shortly made permanent, under the name *Girls' Camp*.

Like Youth House the girls' center has had from the first a supervision both inspired and inspiring. In a memorable series of articles on children in trouble, Albert Deutsch now of the New York *Daily Compass*, wrote this of Girls' Camp: "Seldom have I seen a staff so driven by decent attitudes . . . realistic understanding." Deutsch made the point that girls arrive at the camp "tense and confused . . . helpless and hopeless . . . waiting for something to happen, not knowing what, and building up a defensive devil-may-care attitude. They are susceptible to waves of hysteria. Morale is almost completely shattered. Life seems pointless and aimless. They develop a mask of indifference and even of callousness, to shield themselves from further emotional blows. Girls' Camp receives its charges at a critical moment of their adolescent careers."

And at this moment, the punishments, routines, neglects and distrusts of the average detention home could easily wreak permanent damage, rendering a girl proof against reclamation for the rest of her life. But at Girls' Camp as at Youth House, such cruelties are taboo. In the words of the director, Alice Overton, "For once in her life, the Camper has social status. She finds herself in a society which needs her effort in order to function." For the population is neither pampered nor spoiled. Far from it. They have their daily games and satisfactions—but daily responsibilities as well. Treated with affection, they reciprocate.

Is all light and sweetness at these best of our detention centers? Not by any means. Space is so lacking at Girls' Camp that sleeping quarters must be used as classrooms. Youth House, physically, leaves much to be desired. The inmates are tough and twisted, so that the usual two or three weeks at either home may not prove long enough. Oh, the kids give plenty of trouble, and there are areas enough, assuredly, for possible improvement.

And to show you what so often happens in the detention field, subsiding public interest is already threatening both establishments. Youth House and Girls' Camp, early in 1949, were directed to move. They are actually privately operated by cooperating denominational groups, though the budget is chiefly borne by the city; and it seems that the facilities are required for other uses.

In the end this may turn out for the best. The Community Service Society in its 1949 report urges the city to revamp all detention, setting up a properly constructed central home under the Welfare Department.

Youth House and Girls' Camp, however, have hammered home a lesson:

Juvenile detention, no matter what the local difficulties, need not be one of the "cruel and unusual punishments" banned under the Constitution of the United States!

Maybe that lesson will be taken to heart. Until then America shall remain blemished by a situation thus described in Federal findings concerning detention homes: "Thousands of children a year meet concentrated barrenness, hostility, cruelty and immoral influences—and are confused about what society, the law, the court, really wants for them."

11

Unreformed "Reform"

ALL RIGHT, SO AT LAST THAT TERRIBLE JONES BOY gets out of jail or boarding home, as the case may be. The judge has not been sympathetic, and Jonesy will have to take the cure—about nine months of it.

What happens to him?

A hundred years ago, there would have been only one place for him to go, a House of Refuge on New York's Randall's Island, founded in 1825 by the Society for the Prevention of Juvenile Delinquents.

Today there are "reform" and "correction" facilities aplenty—at least one in every state. They are known among welfare people as "training schools." Jonesy is a Chicago boy, so he is sent to St. Charles—the Illinois State Training School for delinquents.

Jonesy is lucky. This institution, a half-century old, has a brand-new administration. If Jonesy had been sent there only a short while before he would have come under the dubious regime of Col. P. J. Hodgin, appointed superintendent in 1945 by a co-officer in the National Guard. Col. Hodgin's qualifications for the job were two: first, his high-ranking friend happened also to be State Public Welfare Director, and, second, his job in civilian life was that of telephone linesman.

Naturally enough, under a National Guard officer you could count on plenty of "order" at St. Charles. The inmates, 600 of them, were always well-behaved, always quiet. But they walked like zombies! They were in the grip of a monotony as stupefying as dope. If only to break the deadly boredom, every once in a while some kid with more guts than the rest would step out of line—and promptly be sent to the disciplinary quarters, Pierce Cottage. There, if

sullen about it all, he would be stood up naked against a
wall and be given the firehose treatment.

How all this came under the head of training, no one
knew, not even Col. Hodgin. As military discipline, on
knowledge of which the colonel prided himself, it would
have forced revolt from mature men. As a method of giving
boys healthy emotions for morbid ones, of redirecting their
energies and drives into channels acceptable to outside society, it could only fall flat on its face. It would have taught
Jonesy nothing—except, perhaps, that if this was the "good
behavior" he was always hearing about, it was the most
wearisome thing in the world.

But Jonesy, lucky boy, is saved all that. The good colonel was replaced. For a scandal loosed itself. Even over
the radio, thanks to investigation initiated by the inspired
Deutsch articles, the dull, demoralized, discouraged, brow-
beaten condition of St. Charles children was shouted to the
world at large, and to Illinois citizens in particular. Accordingly, the inmates, in 1948, suddenly found themselves
thrown on the more tender mercies of Charles W. Leonard,
a young man renowned for his work with the Catholic
Youth Organization.

So Jonesy can now look forward to a real attempt at rehabilitation. Mr. Leonard is fully aware of the best thinking
on the subject, as expressed by the National Conference on
Prevention and Control of Juvenile Delinquency:

> *Emphasis on education, medical treatment and social
> case work—*
> *Reshaping behavior patterns, achieving healthy emo-
> tional development—*
> *No punitive and retributive notions—*
> *Grouping of delinquents according to attributes—
> special training for various ages, various backgrounds,
> sub-normal and psychotic children, normal and gifted
> children—*

Unaware of these precepts in his behalf, Jonesy finally
arrives at St. Charles, quite impressed by its 600 acres of

green fields and rolling woodland. But he feels nervous and jumpy.

What are they going to do to him?

It takes him some time to find out. A crowd of kids is being admitted along with Jonesy. A lot of hours elapse before his turn comes for a few minutes with a psychologist, who gives him aptitude and intelligence tests.

On the strength of the tests Jonesy finds himself assigned to the laundry shop. Water noises drive him nuts. Ever since his old man drowned. The psychologist might have found that out, if he wasn't so rushed. There's a psychiatrist around too, but he is busy with the psychos included in the new crop of recruits.

Mr. Leonard has compiled a list of psychiatric and case work personnel he hopes to secure, but hasn't yet been able to. "I have complete authority to hire only those qualified," he announces to the papers. "Having qualified people in these posts will give us a fairly good guaranty that a treatment program will eventually develop."

In the laundry, Jonesy balks. Those bubbles and gurgles! A guard comes along—he used to work under Col. Hodgin —takes Jonesy by the ear and dunks his head in a tub. Jonesy grits his teeth and forces himself to work. The guard strolls away. Jonesy throws a flatiron at him.

"I have made no changes in policy or program," says Mr. Leonard, six months after his appointment, "but I have been very careful to observe and evaluate both program and personnel."

For that mixup in the laundry, Jonesy gets transferred. They figure he's a hard case; maybe they can't teach him a trade. He gets put in with other hard cases, supposedly for observation. Jonesy is tough, but some of those guys make his hair stand on end. One always talks to himself. Another, nineteen years old, keeps giggling like a baby. A third guy, says the grapevine, is in on an armed robbery rap.

"We receive many who are sentenced by the criminal or circuit courts . . . we are running both a prison and a training school," says Mr. Leonard. "In addition, our age

span is from ten to twenty-one. This, of course, makes a treatment program practically impotent."

Jonesy himself is seventeen. Quite a sport, outside. Quite a guy with the girls. He misses those girls. He figures there must be saltpeter in the desserts, but it doesn't seem to help much. He never read Kinsey, but he doesn't need professors to tell him that the sex drive in males is strongest between the ages of 16 and 20. He's beginning to lose a lot of sleep. He stays awake nights, waiting for the other guys to conk out so he can "abuse himself" a little. When he does fall asleep, he keeps dreaming about bubbles. By day he is tired and irritable. He gets in a fight with the fellow who talks to himself.

"My basic premise is that juvenile delinquency is now accepted as the symptom of a personality disorder," says Mr. Leonard. "This being true, we must have a mental hygiene unit that will give us as complete a diagnosis as possible and will recommend a treatment program in accord with the individual personality."

When the hell are they going to finish observing him? He wishes he had something to do with himself besides fight with that talking goon. Tension and monotony are breaking him down. He catches a cold. The psychologist gets around for some more tests that day, calls the doctor; Jonesy winds up in the infirmary. After they pump out his nose, he manages to swipe a benzedrine inhaler. Later, he rips it open, chews the loaded paper inside. For two full hours he walks on air—the walls are glass, the sky is technicolor—the talking guy is swell—

That gives him an idea. Some inmates are painting the doors. That night he steals a can of green paint, inhales deeply of the turpentine, sleeps like a baby. But he wakes up in the morning with the heebie-jeebies. He wants air. The windows are barred, but the door stands open and he rushes outside. . . .

An attendant makes a flying tackle, knocking Jonesy down. Automatically, he socks the attendant. He spends the rest of the day in confinement.

"A local newspaper," says Mr. Leonard, "is constantly

exaggerating the number of escapes and making it look as though we are coddling criminals."

It isn't solitary. Nothing like that. All very humane. But he and the other guys locked up sit and twiddle their thumbs, or maybe swap stories. Jonesy is in bad shape. Bubbles all the time. Gurgles. Anyway, he wasn't trying to do anything wrong. What did they lock him up for? The punks! The lousy bastards! All he could think of was his old man sinking. Those bubbles! Jonesy starts to cry. The other guys laugh. Jonesy jumps at them. A calm, efficient attendant hears the noise and stops the fight—fifteen minutes later, with Jonesy half-dead on the floor.

"With personnel so short," says Mr. Leonard, "you can really see that we are doing little more than good custodial work."

And that's the way it goes with Jonesy—till he's a screaming wreck, or the spirit all seeps out of him. . . .

Mr. Leonard is doing his best under difficulties, and makes every member of the staff read his excellent pamphlet on the conduct of the institution, called *Basic Statement of Philosophy*. Albert Deutsch remarks: "If his plans are put into effect, St. Charles may yet become a rehabilitative training school in fact as well as in name."

Meanwhile, what becomes of the Jonesies?

The situation at St. Charles more or less approximates that prevailing at most of our better training schools. The spirit is there, but the flesh is weak. Good intentions remain trammeled by lack of funds, lack of personnel, little sustained public interest—except in jailbreaks—and politics both inside and out. Some institutions see a change of supervision with every switch in elections, as if it makes any difference to children whether they are neglected by Democrats or Republicans.

Yet it cannot be denied that on the whole there is an encouraging tendency away from the punitive and toward the correctional. Today superintendents and staffs, even when they can't do much about it, are pretty widely aware that children in trouble require the most expert psychological handling with emphasis on modern techniques of case and group work. The better methods of reconditioning offenders are in common use, particularly among a few denominational and private welfare projects which operate busy training schools of their own in various states.

Massachusetts, New York, Ohio and others have more and more been taking a leaf out of the experience of these private but quasi-official youth centers and setting up bungalow or residence schools rather than large institutions. Simulating home conditions, these provide a backdrop generally more suitable to rehabilitation. With girls especially the arrangement is successful, for it permits training in domestic affairs of the very kind which will engage them in the outside world. As for the larger institutions, for years these have been tending more toward the "farm" type of community on the one hand, and, on the other, industrial training schools as in Utah and other states. Walls and bars, despite public skittishness with respect to escapes, are on the way out. As put by the authoritative Federal panel on Institutional Treatment, "Surely one of the most effective ways of working toward true reformation is to make the institution setting as unlike a penal station as possible. . . . Children are best trained for freedom in an atmosphere of self-discipline rather than through physical restraints." At a good institution, a few escapes a year are taken for granted. Better to suffer them than risk damaging the rest of the trainees by the psychological implications of prison walls.

All this is the froth at the top, however. It gives an inkling of the aims and ideals, of the better methods, in trying to halt child crime through institutional treatment. In practice, the field is spotty as a Dalmatian pup with the measles.

"An uneven development marked, and still marks, the picture of institutions for erring juveniles in the United States." So states the panel report, published in 1947. Consider the matter of authority alone. The advanced trend, as summed up in the *Social Work Year Book*, "is to make the training school 'an integral part of the total child welfare program' under the jurisdiction of the welfare department

training schools, got replies like these (quoted from the
N. Y. Star, January 6, 1949):

> *"I stood 72 hours handcuffed to a ring."*
> *"I had to do a thousand knee bends or stand on my knees all day."*
> *"First day after I ran away, I marched eight hours a day around a basement and ate meals standing up. I continued to march 30 days."*
> *". . . Locked in a cell with bread and water for 60 days."*
> *"Got 175 licks with a hose loaded with copper cable for running away."*
> *"Took off my shoes . . . beat my feet with a strap till they were black and blue."*

Albert Deutsch further reports visiting a southern training school which operates a "bull ring." Here boys are punished by being made to walk or run around a set of posts,
carrying heavy packs on their backs. Sentences would be
for 500 hours or more, to be worked off on Sundays. In the
same state at another school, two boys were placed in solitary confinement in unheated rooms. It can get pretty cold
in the higher areas of the South! The boys developed frost-
bite, and had to have parts of their feet amputated.

The Children's Bureau quotes one broadly-experienced
reform school superintendent on corporal punishment: "Too
dangerous. Too few people blessed with enough judgment
to use it—those so blessed don't need it." Yet the most recent panel report is obliged to state:

> Corporal punishment and other abuses are still far too
> prevalent. Among the disciplinary practices in training
> schools, reported by reliable observers, are the following:
> whipping or spanking with sticks, wire coat hangers, pad-
> dles, straps; striking about the face and head with fists
> and stocks; handcuffing to the bed at night; use of shack-
> les and leg chains; shaving of the head; cold tubbings;
> 'standing on the line' in a rigid position for hours at a

time; confinement in dark cells and dungeonlike basement rooms; silence rules; knee bends; a modified lock-
step in marching formations; permitting boy monitors to
discipline other boys with corporal punishment. Particularly vicious is the monitor system, which permits older,
more aggressive children to exert authority over the more
timid and less mature.

"All children learn more quickly by reward and encouragement than by punishment," warns the same report. "Desirable conduct is motivated through positive, constructive
means." Another investigation, weighing pros and cons of
corporal punishment in juvenile training school, decides:
"Under intelligent and humane personnel, boys and girls
can be controlled without it. Corporal punishment tends
not only to brutalize those upon whom it is inflicted, but
also those who inflict it."

For proof, if it is needed, of the effectiveness of more
humane methods, we see that even the most informal control can achieve startling results. Some of the most successful of the newer training projects are no more than camps.
No elaborate prison plant, no walls, no locked buildings,
no solitary cells—but relatively small groups of adolescents, developing social responsibility and self-reliance in a
healthy outdoor setting.

The outstanding example, perhaps, is the camp for boy
delinquents operated by the Federal Bureau of Prisons in
Virginia. Discipline, morale and genuine social responsibility flourish through a boy-to-counselor and boy-to-group
relationships similar to those in any summer camp. Escapes? Some. But why should a boy in his right mind want
to leave such a place? Results? Boys learn what decency is,
and are given the means to achieve it.

The camp idea is being given vigorous development in
California. A forestry camp was first opened by the Los
Angeles probation department in 1931 to handle the large
numbers of transient youth constantly encountered on the
west coast. Later, five more camps were established, and all
reorientated to handle delinquent boys. In 1941, the state

set up the California Youth Authority to handle its growing delinquency problem, under the direction of the man origi-nally responsible for the Los Angeles camp—Karl Holton. Under his sponsorship, camps or camplike facilities have been installed in considerable number. Cooperating locali-ties including San Francisco have also set up camps. The system is far from perfect—chiefly, according to Mr. Hol-ton, because of lack of good personnel. But results have been good. Minnesota, Wisconsin, Massachusetts and other states are experimenting with similar camps.

The California Youth Authority is one of the more en-lightened answers to the challenge of delinquency. Governor Warren, at the time it was created, ranked it "among the greatest social experiments." By authority of the legislature, it has broad, independent powers to create and supervise all anti-delinquency activity. Yet so confused, so uneven, so difficult is training school reform, that in California, as elsewhere, little headway is being made.

The state training schools at Whittier and Preston, and the one for girls at Ventura, present the usual uninspiring picture of deadly routine, repression, prisonlike atmos-phere. At the Preston School of Industry, boys are organ-ized on a military system reminiscent of Col. Hodgin's, with the hundreds of inmates subject to rigid and gratingly mo-notonous discipline. Whittier is supposed to be improving under a new and highly qualified director. So is Ventura, also under new management.

Certainly the 200 girls at Ventura no longer walk around with their heads shaved, forbidden to talk to one another, as once they had to do. Spankings are not resorted to, as they still are in many girls' reform schools. Solitary confine-ment is not prescribed at the drop of a hat, as, say in the Geneva girls' school of Illinois. Girls, by way of punish-ment, are not forced to parade naked before the inmates as in at least one state reform school reported in the press. Corporal punishment is not officially permitted, as, for ex-ample at Claremont, the Indiana girls' school. Silence rules or such measures as being deprived of desserts are the com-mon punishments for minor infractions at Ventura. Serious offenders are dealt with by banishment to disciplinary cottages—a common practice the country over, in good schools and bad.

But as "training," as education for an adjusted life in the outside world, the Ventura program leaves much to be desired. It is in this area, indeed, that training schools fall down most seriously. Here—and in the deadly, monotonous regimentation which all too often passes for program.

How can this be otherwise, with shortages of good personnel as universal as they are?

So-called teachers are often mere workmen around an institution, who, if they happen to be plumbers, supervise boys assigned to plumbing. Staff educational preparation is deplorable—this despite the fact that training a case-hardened delinquent is one of the most ticklish of educational tasks, challenging the ingenuity and knowledge of the most skilled teacher.

The widely hailed White House Conference on child welfare, which set up a kind of bill of rights for the kids of this land, includes in it the basic premise that every child— *every* child—is entitled to such education as he can sustain. That is solid American principle. For the health of this Democracy, for the permanence of this Republic, kids between 6 and 16 must go to school.

But in ten sample training schools surveyed by the U. S. Office of Education, teachers—and often unqualified teachers, at that—handled an average of sixty-three pupils each. "Classes" consisting of the most difficult and challenging problems in education, hard enough to cope with even by individual instruction, sometimes ran to more than a hundred kids per teacher!

Surveys by the Osborne Association (headed by Austin McCormick, former Correction Commissioner of New York) —by Ohio State University—by the Federal Children's Bureau—by the Office of Education—all point to the same conclusion. If the training aim is to be realized, "there must be drastic changes in the educational practices" of reform schools. And before this can come about, before good and sufficient teachers, attendants and professional staff can become available, there must be even more drastic changes in "attitudes of the public, educators and legislators toward the educational functions of training schools." In other words, the sights must be raised. And appropriations.

Ventura, with all its faults, stands well up with the best of the girls' schools. Yet, as of this writing, even Ventura, for all the good intentions of the California Youth Authority, does not boast a psychiatrist. Psychiatrists are scarce, numbering fewer than 5000 in this country—and many of these of questionable training. With millions of respectable, if neurotic, Americans to be serviced, why should the psychiatrist bury his talents in a home for wayward girls who probably are a total loss anyway?

Well, maybe he shouldn't. Maybe it pays better to let him give priority to honest citizens. It certainly pays *him* better.

But experts, including those comprising the Attorney General's advisory group on the subject, believe that most psychiatric problems of the juvenile delinquent can be ably handled by the social case worker, the social group worker, and the psychologist. Of these there are a goodly number in our country—but not on the premises of reform schools. In the opinion of a blasphemous few, a clinical psychologist can generally do more good, practical repair work on a young delinquent than can the psychoanalytical type of psychiatrist. The psychologist tends to work like the doctor to whom you take your broken arm, he judges the fracture, makes tests for its size and location, sets it on the spot with such splints as he may have.

The psychoanalyst would ask you where you broke it and when, whether anybody saw you break it, and how come you were foolish enough to go around fracturing yourself; suicidal tendencies, no doubt.

This is no place to weigh professional methodologies: the sole point is that almost any therapy may help the delinquent—but the people to give therapy are missing. Even at institutions which do boast a few qualified professionals, the case load is so heavy that the psychologist, say, functions merely as a psychometrist. He gives tests. Intelligence tests, personality tests, skill tests. But true clinical psychology, as such, is almost never practiced in the country's reform schools.

One of the most famous reformatories in the world does boast a full-time psychiatrist and not one, but two psychologists. This is a reformatory, not a reform school, you understand. The inmates, while under twenty-one on admittance, are almost all graduates of reform schools who have been convicted for second or third offenses. It has a population of 1200.

Wearying of the endless routine of giving tests and assigning jobs to newly admitted offenders, one of the psychologists proposed that he take his psychology "out into the prison." He wanted to travel around the cells and shops, take notes on how well the inmates were doing in their assigned jobs. He wanted to study them at work, at play, during sleep. He wanted to compile more complete records about the behavior of the inmate during his stay. He thought that in this fashion he might be able to help some of the boys. His suggestions were quickly shouted down at the weekly meeting of the reformatory administration.

Was he criticizing the supervision? Wasn't he satisfied with the work of his immediate boss, the psychiatrist? Who did he think he was, Freud? Why, the chief keeper was a better psychologist than a fellow who had merely read some books. The keeper could take new inmates, look at them once, and seventy percent of the time guess just what offense they had been committed for. Brother, that was really psychologizing! The assistant superintendent was so angry that he swore he would have the upstart, a civil service appointee, transferred or fired within the month. "But I remained a year and a half," the psychologist told us. "The reformatory superintendent kept me around just to irritate his assistant!"

Which provides a clue to another of the weaknesses in reform practice today; bitter internecine politics. Any probation or correction worker can tell of jealousies, bickering and quarrels which ruin staff morale, kill homogeneity, destroy enthusiasm in some of the better training schools and cottages. The work is hard and thankless, the pay is poor, the plums are few: in many states employes serve without tenure, without security, without supervision competent enough to appreciate it when they do turn in a good job.

Under such conditions, how can we expect the democratization which occurs in the California delinquency camps, for instance, but in few other public reform projects? Practice in dynamic social adjustment, in participating with the group, has been recognized by the Children's Bureau, the Federal Prison Administration and other competent authorities as essential to juvenile reclamation. Ditto for acquisition by the child of a feeling of his own value, his own contribution, to the society around him. He belongs! Through his contribution and its acceptance he acquires in his own eyes what every person needs as a bulwark against sinning: a sense of dignity, obligation, self-respect. Ruinous to this essential democratization are the regimentation and iron repression converting so many of our training schools into concentration camps.

Equally ruinous is any carry-over of ignorance and prejudice from the outside world. *Intolerance in any shape reflects a weakness in authority which in the end must flaw still more seriously the already damaged personality of the delinquent.* Yet what do we learn from Federal Security Agency figures? The very states which have the largest Negro populations have the fewest training facilities for Negro delinquents—sometimes none at all. And a large number of institutions, north as well as south, maintain separate or segregated facilities only.

The statistics also reveal the origin of a libel. It is widely accepted that non-white children are more inclined to delinquency than white. Yes, in training schools you will find some 29 percent of the children to be non-white, whereas non-whites comprise but 13 percent of the general population. But, states the Federal report, this merely reflects the inadequacy of private training and welfare facilities for colored children.

Regimentation and prejudice, in the world of reform schools, seem to go together. Especially in some girls' schools, where the democratic process, the principles of human dignity, seem even less in evidence than among boys' institutions. It has been guessed that this often derives from the prissiness of the dried-up old maids commonly in charge, most of whom have never known temptation, let alone love.

The New York State Training School for Girls and a number of others admit Negro girls. But at most schools strict segregation is the rule.

Albert Deutsch reports a typical justification for segregation coming from Elizabeth H. Lewis, superintendent of the Geneva school in Illinois:

"White and Negro girls in this type of institution tend to 'honey up' to one another when they are mixed in common living quarters. That is, they tend to develop homosexual crushes for those of the opposite racial group. Then again, Negro girls just like to be with their own, just as white girls do."

That business of "liking to be with their own" needs little comment. Scientific evidence as ironclad as a battleship proves that children never show color prejudice until taught to do so.

But what about the old charge that the creamy and the brown make a seductive blend? This is one of the most persistent legends in the literature of penology. Is there any truth in it?

As a matter of fact, any average group of Negro girls will show certain handsome, well-proportioned types, sexually ripe in terms of physical development, and with a contagious vitality, a vigor, which further enriches their nubility. As sexual objects, they would appear to surpass in pure sensual attraction most white girls of similar age. This may simply be a function of earlier sexual maturity. It follows that if a homosexual were casting about for a conquest, it might be guessed that she would by choice set her cap for one of these velvet-skinned girls. And the latter, being sexually precocious, might be expected to respond ardently once desire was aroused. Additionally, there is the fact that dif-

ference in color adds exotic attraction, at least in the esti-
mation of the experienced homosexual. In homosex as in
heterosex, variety is the spice.

Yet girls in institutions show only a fractionally greater
incidence of congenital or homosexual-by-choice specimens
than does the population at large. This may mean that the
prime reason for homosexuality in training school is not pre-
disposition, but lack of access to the opposite sex. Hence, in
her homosexual experiences, the girl attempts to duplicate
the appearances and satisfactions of heterosexual ones. In
short, she wants to be stroked, kissed and handled by somebody as male as possible.

Now, young Negro girls are apt to exhibit muscular con-
formations more like that of males: biceps, for instance,
tend to be more developed than among white girls. Often
the buttocks, when lean, have a manly hardness; when fat,
instead of spreading in womanly fashion they project rear-
ward as among boys. Add to this a physical vigor and
darker color which may heighten the illusion of male viril-
ity, and it is not strange that where homosexuality exists, a
Negro girl is often the prize. By the same token, the Negro
girl finds in the desire and surrender of this pale girl a titillating circumstance, and one flattering to her self-esteem.
She responds by lavishing such love and protection as she
can.

There is truth, then, in the oft-repeated charge that
mixing prison populations raises the incidence of "honeying-up"? Perhaps. This author has not investigated the
question.

But training schools and detention homes are not prisons.
Judging by the very scant figures available from punishment records and in-service reports—by talks with girl
"graduates"—by information from in-service social and
psychiatric workers—one conclusion seems valid enough.
Mixed institutions show less—actually less—homosexuality
than do segregated ones. How much less? Generally not a
significant amount, for wherever girls gather in isolation
under the tutelage of elder women—including certain colleges, sororities and boarding schools—homosexuality is in-

clined to take hold. But the charge that misconduct is caused by the mere mixing of color stocks does not appear to hold water.

The truth is that whatever the sexual desire one girl of different hue may arouse in another, it is directed toward an individual—not the color group. Certain girls, endowed physically or emotionally, are prizes. Often they are Negro girls. But in their absence there would be no foregoing of homosexual activity.

It would merely be directed elsewhere, toward such white girls as might happen to be available.

Non-segregation, on the other hand, while itself having no effect on the incidence of sex offenses, often reflects a more enlightened and liberalized training school policy. This translates itself into less tedium, less repression, more diversion and outlet for girlish energies.

In turn, a lowering in frequency of offenses may occur as a result.

Formerly, though not so extensively now, in northern unsegregated prisons the Negro girl came heavily under the impact of racial discrimination. She was contemptuously imposed upon in all ways by the rest of the prison population, including homosexuals. One visiting prison psychiatrist in Indiana suggests that the Negro girl would later get revenge on the "superior" race, and at the same time appease her sexual appetites, by seducing young white girls. Having become skilled in techniques, moreover, she could arouse these girls to ardent cravings which gave her a feeling of power compensating for her "inferiority." Whatever this explanation is worth, at a guess it is from such origins that the stubborn slander arose which still prevails at places like Geneva.

Investigations of prison homosexualism have been few. Generally they came from analysts of the Freudian or Jungian variety, and apart from coming up with conclusions hardly significant in the light of more modern approaches, they were at fault in doing little to lay the ghost of mixed "honeying-up." Others perpetuated it on the basis of hearsay.

Dr. Maurice Chideckel, in one of the few published discussions of the problem contained in his *Female Sex Perversion*, went so far as to concentrate almost exclusively on relations between white and Negro women, as if in institutions others were rarely guilty.

Thus distorted has been the whole matter of perversion in training schools, boys' as well as girls'. Huge areas are dark. Little or no research goes on. Handling of the respective local situations is largely up to the whim and outlook of the administrative officer—possibly an ignorant "keeper." Here is one of the greatest—least discussed—of all the numerous problems facing juvenile correction authorities.

Some superintendents wink at homosexualism. "What can you expect?" Others sternly repress it by isolations, beatings or other cruelties. In nearly every training school, counter-aphrodisiac chemicals are served in the food, but rarely live up to their reputations. No one knows the real percentages of illicit love. Among boys, however, it would seem to be far less prevalent than among girls. Your typical adolescent is interested primarily in release, which can be achieved through masturbation and emission. Further, even under powerful sex urges, as a rule a boy regards with repugnance any intimate contact with his own sex, indulges only with shame.

But with girls more is involved than orgasm or release. There exists a whole "crush" pattern stemming from the need to bestow and receive affection. The adolescent girl requires love—and its overt manifestation, such as embracing. Moreover, girls do not usually find their own sex physically repugnant. They are accustomed from childhood to kiss, pat, hug, fondle and hold hands with other girls. Hence, given contributing circumstances, they are more prone to slip into homosexual relationships than are boys.

Among girls or boys under cottage or camp conditions, homosexualism is not more a problem than it would be in a similar environment in the "normal" world. Physical energies are used up by work and play, close supervision is possible through cottage "parents" or camp "counselors," and, above all, children in different age groups are kept apart. Under repressed, monotonous routine and more or less indiscriminate age-mixing in larger institutions, however, the tragedy is that the younger children learn from or are seduced by their elder co-delinquents. Even where homosexualism is strictly proscribed and the most elaborate precautions taken, it stubbornly persists. Amazing is the ingenuity and persistence shown in getting around restrictions, especially by older girls.

"Give these institutionalized persons credit," writes Dr. Chideckel. "They are never dismayed by failure. Even among higher types, as in convents and girls' schools where the most drastic measures of repression are instituted to prevent the carrying on of homosexuality, prodigious intellectual feats are displayed to mislead the supervisors. The confraternity formed among these pseudo-homosexuals, their alertness against the danger of being detected, their ways of breaking through the barriers that hem them in, are in themselves a psychological study. Beneath the crass surface, under the watchful eyes of the guards, a life is stirring, unobserved and unknown."

Queried as to how she achieved her pleasures, one miss of sixteen, known to be spreading homosexual practice in a tightly controlled training school, replied:

"It's no good at night. Too many in the dormitory. At salute (flag assembly each morning) I line up behind Marty. We're all crowded together. I just sort of rub against her."

"That satisfies you?"

"Better than nothing. She's so nice. I wish I could hug her and kiss her! They don't let you."

Here is another story:

"They don't let you get away with a thing at this joint. I knew the supervisor was no "friend" [homosexual] but she was my only chance. I kept looking at her and smiling at her. I gave her a cake my sister sent me, my birthday. You're not allowed to touch supervisors, but I got her to thinking I liked her. She didn't mind it when I sort of touched her sometimes. Like when she was handing me something, I touched her hand. Or her leg. When I could, I kept letting her see me. Sitting down, I'd spread my legs or bend over. Thursdays we line up for scrub. If she was on duty, I would sing, stretch myself and kind of look at her, waddle around, anything so she'd notice me, especially under the shower. The girls figured I was polishing her for favors. I really worked on her. I'm telling you. Four months before I got a bite.

"Supervisors sleep just outside the coops, get it? They take turns at each coop. During the month she was at ours, I yelled out in the middle of the night. When she ran in I told her I was sick. I said if I could only get to the toilet I'd be all right. She helped me, and I acted like I was dying, hanging on to her and squeezing for dear life. When I came out I told her, if I could only see my mother. Would she give me a goodnight hug, like my mother?

"You could have knocked me over! The old battleaxe said yes. She felt sorry for me or something. I hugged her. I felt funny. I started to cry. She sat down and took me on her lap and patted me. I kept my face on her breasts like I was still crying. After that when I used to smile at her she began to smile back. Then one night I knocked on her door and said would she let me hug her like before. She said yes. She held me on her lap a long time. I wriggled around until she said what did I think I was doing?

"The next day I got up my nerve. I said I wanted to tell her something. I said I was kind of ashamed taking scrub with all the other girls. I said I never really got a wash, everybody rushing you and standing around watching you. I could tell that she didn't really believe me. But she said okay, except that she would have to supervise. In the shower I strutted around and sang. I put soap all over and said, Gee if only someone would wash my back. She was looking at me funny. She said well, she didn't mind. She took off her clothes and got into the shower. I squeezed up to her. Suddenly she began kissing my hair— I knew she was a dead duck."

"You have relationships with this supervisor now?"

"Yes."

"You like her, is that it? You love her and need her?"

"Love her! That skinny, old battleaxe? I was just soften-ing her up. Now we have nice parties when she's on coop duty. She doesn't say a word, otherwise I wouldn't give her what she wants from me! Listen, lady, I bet a couple of kids would have killed themselves if it wasn't for me loving them and helping them. . . ."

"But you'll be out of here in three months. Was it worth the trouble?"

"What else is there to do? It's the only thing that means anything, or that you can get a kick out of."

Although the forms taken are highly individualized and seem dictated by opportunity and circumstance rather than any general predilection for one method or another, it may be said that on the whole among juveniles no true homo-sexual exchange takes place. With both boys and girls, the common practice is mutual masturbation and mutual han-dling. Cunnilingual and other more vigorous exchanges characterizing patent homosexualism would appear to be practiced by older girls almost exclusively. With these the practice can develop in its most vicious forms.

Now, the question of vice in training schools is far from simple. There are those who argue that as a kind of catalytic for the growth of "love" and the exchange of "affection," and as a simple release, it does more good than harm. They do not condemn unnatural sex in institutionalized circum-stances simply because such sex is condemned in free cir-cumstances; by this view, what is considered "unnatural" becomes, behind institutional walls, the "natural." Others believe that since training school populations are all com-posed of adolescents, they can well do without sex—indeed, are supposed to. Certainly, as the Kinsey Report and other studies have shown, among males enormous sex potentials and drives exist at these ages. About sex impulses in girls, less is known. Yet the incidence of masturbation, affairs, seductions, out-of-wedlock babies and even marriages among girls below sixteen, let alone those older, would lead us to believe that perhaps they are not so far behind boys in their sexual needs as society and law would have us think.

Yet we must remember that the training school adolescent is not condemned for life. He is being trained, specifically, to rejoin normal society within a relatively short period. If so, no matter what reasons or excuses can be advanced for tolerating homosexuality, it is defeating the very purpose of the institution; it renders the inmate "abnormal." Intro· duced to the aberration at an early, impressionable age, he is likely to bear its stamp forever.

It is not necessary to discuss whether homosexualism, as such, should be punished or not, is good or bad, is natural or unnatural with certain individuals, is to be pitied, condoned, accepted. We merely make the point that in the society which the institutionalized delinquent is to rejoin, homosexualism is vigorously frowned on. It is considered anti-social. It is a definite aberration, and the delinquent is supposed to be institutionalized so that he may be freed of aberrations. Another point: as Dr. O. Spurgeon English of Temple University writes in *About the Kinsey Report*, "Homosexuals usually meet with social rebuff, ostracism, if their true nature becomes known. If it is kept secret, they have all the problems which arise from an individual's attempt to conceal an important part of himself and live in a world apart." That is, the delinquent released with a homosexual habit has even less chance of normal adjustment to society than before he entered.

Dr. English also reminds us:

"To condemn homosexuality will never accomplish anything. Its elimination lies in finding the most healthy and wholesome expression of sexuality for all, and that will come only when we cease being afraid of sex. . . . If we are disturbed by the incidence, we should ask ourselves how this kind of behavior is brought about and how it can be prevented."

The doctor is writing of homosexualism generally, not of homosexualism in training schools. His point is that more attention should be paid to the abnormal factors in a child's environment which may culminate in making him a "fairy" or a "dyke." How much more this message applies to the young occupants of training schools! *All* sexual factors in their institutionalized environment are abnormal. As for the questions he raises, the answers are explicit enough. *"The most healthy and wholesome expression of sexuality?"*—between boy and girl, obviously. *"How is homosexual behavior brought about?"*—by segregating boy and girl. *"How can it be prevented?"*—by unsegregating them.

QUESTION: Could the cure, then, lie in making reform schools coeducational?

ANSWER: In the opinion of many, including your author —yes!

Eleven coeducational reform schools, indeed, are actually operating in the United States.

Only a few allow any mutual projects, except for children under twelve. In the majority, by coeducation is meant simply the existence of rigidly separated schools for boys and girls within the confines of the same institution.

Sex incidents? Less frequent than at the high school in your town.

Homosexualism? Almost unheard of, in those of the institutions about which your author has been able to get information.

The faintest aura—the distant, occasional glimpse—the mere knowledge of nearness—any of these seem enough, where both sexes are countenanced in one institution, to withhold sex drives from the unnatural. We spoke to one boy on parole from Hampton Farms, a correctional school in New York State. He was a consistent offender, and had been in several institutions, sometimes for sentences of over a year. His remarks were instructive:

"After you serve long enough, you forget all about girls. You don't even remember how they look. You don't feel sexy or anything. You don't think about it. You don't think about anything. Just a long, dull grind. But every once in a while—well, if a kid on the next bed undresses, and he has a pink skin or something, it looks awful good to you.

"When girls are around somewhere, do you see them?

Maybe once a month, like if you're promoted to the library. But you know they're there. Things even get through the grapevine, real romance, and how you're going to chase this one or that when your stretch is up. You think of your sisters, maybe some of the girls you had. Okay, so you get hot once in a while. So you dream it off. Or [masturbate]. You don't go looking at no boys in the next bed."

Concerning coeducational training schools—not simply separate boys' and girls' schools on the same grounds, but actual coeducational institutions, the National Conference on Prevention and Control of Juvenile Delinquency has this to say:

"Some leading correctional authorities feel there is sound basis for the belief that training schools should be on a co-educational basis if they are to teach the boys and girls who are sent to them how to live in accordance with acceptable social standards, and especially if they are to be taught to comprehend and accept a proper relationship with the opposite sex, a lesson many of them need to learn more than anything else. It is bad enough to have to remove adolescent boys and girls from normal community life at the very time when they need to be associating with children of both sexes under wholesome conditions and proper guidance. It is doubly bad to put them, then, into an unnatural, segregated environment that intensifies the very problems it is meant to solve."

The Federal panel report advises that if a training school is to care for both girls and boys, "The sexes must be well-balanced in number so that the interests of neither group are subordinated and sex-consciousness is not intensified. The program must be genuinely coeducational, moreover, with the same type of supervised activities and contact that one would find in a good residential school anywhere." It warns further that "the chief obstacle to successful operation appears to be public opinion. If newspapers are to attack the school, if the public is to become apprehensive and critical because 'bad boys and girls' are being allowed to associate with each other, and if the superintendent's dismissal is to be demanded whenever a boy and girl behave improperly, it is not best to establish a coeducation program and see it go down to failure."

For the latter reason, the panel does an abrupt about-face. "After careful consideration, the panel concludes that the coeducational system is not practical and is not recommended."

Another defeat for reclaiming "the most difficult and maladjusted children of our communities."

And so, while slow progress is being made on many fronts, the only possible conclusion about training schools is that by and large they are doing more harm than good. The trainee leaves them, more often than not, worse off than when he entered. Reform school graduates, as J. Edgar Hoover has pointed out, show a hopeless number of recidivists who grow up into our worst and most inveterate criminals.

We have seen that in the training institution field, these improvements are most needed:

1. Divorce from politics, and centralization of authority in specialized, preferably welfare, personnel.
2. Qualified and plentiful psychiatric, psychological and teaching staffs.
3. Gradual elimination of large units in favor of small ones, particularly of the "camp" or "bungalow" type.
4. Replacement of corporal punishment and repression by humanized programming motivating and developing the trainee as a social being.
5. Coeducation, or some substitute supplying occasional social contact between boy and girl.

Plenty of room for improvement in other directions, too. But the above items will do for the present. If and when they are even partially achieved by a majority of our training schools, the institutionalized delinquent will become less a social casualty and more a potential asset, if not to humanity, then at least to himself.

12

Anticipating Delinquency

MANY ATTEMPTS HAVE BEEN MADE TO PIN DOWN scientifically the causes of delinquency. To date, these researches have yielded few concrete results, and these often contradictory. Despite the occasional claim of this sociologist or that psychiatrist that he has discovered the true "key" to delinquency, the fact is that no single factor or set of factors has been isolated which, when found in child or adolescent, is always, or even frequently, accompanied by delinquent patterns.

In this respect, one child's meat is another child's poison. That is, the very personality traits which in John make him a young criminal may in Mary make a lass exceptionally valuable to her community.

Take "aggressiveness," so often mentioned as a defining characteristic of the delinquent. By virtue of heredity, conditioning, frustration or what have you, John at fifteen is exceptionally aggressive. So is Mary, the same age, one of his classmates at public school.

John's outlet for aggressiveness is the beating up of the nearest person at hand. He is not a bully, for he takes on boys much larger than himself, or even teachers. He also pummels girls and younger children. He uses his fists, with which he has developed great skill, but is just as likely to strike with sticks, stones or anything else at hand. In short, he is completely and indiscriminately aggressive. Not unnaturally, this has rendered him hopelessly unpopular, which in turn makes him more aggressive still. He has been in frequent conflict with school authorities and police. Recently he walked into the office of his principal and demanded that he be transferred from the class of a teacher he disliked. The principal refused. John took a gun out of his pocket and fired two shots at the principal's head. Both missed, but one buried itself in the arm of the school clerk. John is now thinking things over at a state farm.

What of Mary? She too is aggressive, inclined to strike anybody in sight unless she has her way. So much so that one day this hoyden sneaked up behind John and knocked him unconscious with a baseball bat! This brought her instant popularity; in a wave of gratitude, her fellows elected her president of the school student body. Did this make her less aggressive? Hardly. Indeed, her newfound position simply meant more opportunity to throw her weight about, with the result that she became more obnoxious than ever. One day, with the authority of her position and her super-aggressiveness behind her, she brazenly bearded the director of the school lunchroom. The food, said Mary, stank. "These sandwiches! What do you do, buy bargains!" The answer of the director failed to satisfy. Whereupon Mary threw her salmon sandwich at him, plus the plate it had been on.

Properly reprimanded for the transgression, Mary took steps. So aggressive, don't you know? She pummeled even the more timid members of her class into writing complaints about the school food. Armed with these letters, she sought the mayor of her town. Probably she would have pummeled him too, but she couldn't get in to see him. She promptly sent the letters to a local newspaper.

The director had been buying bargains, all right. A scandal broke. Food at the lunchroom rapidly improved. And Mary found victory, like the new brand of salmon, quite to her taste. She launched a number of fresh campaigns with the enforced cooperation of her schoolmates. Today, thanks to her, the school gym boasts a new coat of paint, and remains open evenings to keep kids like herself and John out of trouble. The townsfolk look on Mary as a leader of youth, and while still as aggressive as ever, she is learning to use wiles and words instead of fists.

These events took place in a small midwest city. They demonstrate, as do thousands upon thousands of other cases, the almost hopeless difficulty of determining just what causes delinquency. Certainly, aggressive tendencies lead numerous youths into delinquent behavior. So do slum life, repression, frustration, parental neglect and all the rest of the "causes" to which it is so frequently attributed.

But the aggressive child, as we all know, may do himself and his community great good as well as bad. The slum child may rise to be an Al Smith and the impoverished one, a Lincoln. The repressed one, whatever his inner conflicts may be all the more "civilized" thereby—strictly inhibiting all acts frowned on by society. The child frustrated in one direction may all the more strongly seek expression in another, good as well as bad. As for parental neglect, many children become delinquents though carefully enough reared; although, truly enough, such neglect apparently comes closer to being a common cause of delinquency than any other, it is all a matter of degree and circumstance.

In short, the very trait which is so objectionable in one boy proves a blessing in another. The very circumstance which breaks Molly is the making of Polly.

Further, it would seem that the causes of delinquency are not only obscure; they are legion. Take the blames cited in a given case. The policeman says "bad companions." The judge says "neglect by the authorities." The case worker says "poor home environment." The psychologist says "retardation due to low I.Q." The teacher says "improper motivation." The physician says "poor nutrition." The psychiatrist says "paranoiac tendencies." The sociologist says "shallow cultural background." The psychoanalyst, bless him, after seven months of probing, decides: "He hates his father as a rival for the love of his mother, and takes it out on society, which to him is the father-symbol, except when it is the mother-symbol."

No doubt there is ample truth in the conclusions of each of these experts, which, after all, arise from years of close and often shrewd observation. If so, this only serves to emphasize the complexity of the delinquency syndrome!

Little wonder that investigators have made such scant progress in isolating scientifically reliable causal factors! How proceed among the welter of observed symptoms, effects and "causes," sometimes occurring in conjunction with one another and sometimes not—sometimes altogether absent—sometimes seated in personality traits, sometimes in environment, sometimes in both? Do these reduce to a common denominator? Or should such investigations be given up—since the task appears so slow, involved and doubtful of issue—and stress confined to defending society against the delinquent by punishing him, by isolating him in prison where he can't harm anybody?

To this, obviously, the answer must be no. Research aimed at first causes should not be abandoned, but redoubled. For if indeed the predetermining factors of delinquency could be defined adequately, far more effective "preventative medicine" would be possible, replacing the well-meant but scattergun efforts generally relied on today. And though the job, as we have seen, is highly complex and difficult, it is by no means hopeless. The obstacles would appear to lie more in the attitudes of those concerned with the problem than in the actual complications of the research.

In large cities, for example, surprisingly little love is lost between case workers and teachers. Time and again this author has heard teachers say, "Hmph! Working on their own time. Nothing to do all day but walk around and visit folks when they feel like it." Whereas the case worker, forgetting that the teacher has all she can do to pound some reading, arithmetic and character-training into large groups of restless rascals, bitterly complains: "Why doesn't she give little maladjusted Henry more attention? Why doesn't she keep in closer contact with his home, give him more work really suited to him?" Probably the corner cop invokes a plague on both their houses. "Ought to lock that Henry up. A bad example, and he's damaging property!" Similarly, the clinical psychologist, engrossed in tests and personality scales, scorns what he considers the outworn techniques of the analyst. Whether or not he is right, the point is that all participating in the fight against delinquency should preserve open minds, cooperative hearts, and eyes free from wool. They should not wall themselves off one from the other, should not regard any one approach or psychological school as sacred.

When the problem is approached objectively—and by persons of adequate training using modern techniques—genuine progress toward ending the confusion prevailing in the delinquency field is not impossible. A case in point is a study by Wallace Ludden published in *School and Society*, concerned with anticipating juvenile delinquency in a child before it actually occurs. Investigations of this subject both more recent and more exhaustive are on the record. Nevertheless, his is exemplary in approach and method.

The Ludden experiment did not make the mistake of trying to get at basic causes all in one jump. It attempted, rather, to identify such phenomena as might be constant in the delinquency pattern. Only in such phenomena could a clue to omnipresent cause be found. Besides, this had its strong practical side. If characteristics once established as definitely associated with delinquency could be uncovered in a child not yet delinquent, it might be possible to rescue him from a life of crime before he even began it.

The study is prefaced by the often-heard remark that if delinquency continues to spread, our children may well lose us the peace and sweep away America's whole social heritage. Check! It continues to the effect that while professionals, courts and volunteer workers are at work on the problem, they deal chiefly with children already delinquent, already more or less fixed in habit. Check again!

It states that it would be mighty helpful if there were some practical method to determine which children were headed for trouble, a method applicable in the schools, since apparently such children's homes were failing them. Once these kids were filtered out, therapeutic attention could be concentrated on them before their habits were permanently formed. Double-check, Mr. Ludden!

For practicality, the ideal method would derive from information generally on file in school systems, this investigator felt. Recourse to special tests or case study techniques would require specialists available only in a limited number of places. Accordingly, he worked only from the ordinary school records kept in New York, the state where the experiment was conducted.

These records are of three kinds: 1. scholastic achieve-ment 2. health 3. census. Choosing a city whose proportion of foreign-born and foreign-antecedent population approximated the average for the United States, he selected a total of 345 delinquents—children in the seventh, eighth or ninth grades who had incurred police action for violating the law. For a control group he selected from the same grades 641 boys and girls at random.

Next, from the record cards, he summarized the data for the delinquents as of one term preceding the date of each one's fall from grace. Data for the control, or non-delinquent, group he summarized as of the date the study was made. Significance of each factor was determined statistically, by the well-known device of critical ratios. Here is what he found, with the critical ratio appearing next to each factor:

TABLE I—*Facts on record cards associated with known delinquency, and therefore presumed to be indicative of possible delinquency*

	Critical Ratio
1. Living in an area where delinquency is common	9.1
2. Chronologically over age for grade	8.88
3. Living in low rent area	8.40
4. Living in broken homes	7.50
5. Different homes lived in, if more than one	6.76
6. Poor school attendances—over five absences	6.43
7. Terms repeated, more than one	6.40
8. School failures, more than one subject	6.49
9. Terms with failing marks, two or more	5.61
10. Intelligence below 90 (Otis)	4 to 6
11. Low employment continuity of father	4.72
12. Tardiness at school (any)	4.65
13. Illegal absences over five	4.32
14. Intermediate position in sibling group	2.10

TABLE II—*Facts unfavorable to delinquency*

1. Chronologically young for grade	7.02
2. Intelligence above 100 (Otis)	5 plus
3. Youngest child in family	2.80
4. Mothers stay home as housewives	2.10

Note that the indicated ratios reveal little chance error involved. Just the same, Mr. Ludden found his results disappointing. Some 69 percent of his delinquent group did score three or more of the "delinquency" factors, but so did more than 25 percent of the non-delinquents. Were one in four of the control group, then, headed for crime and arrest? Clearly this figure was too high. And what of the 31 percent of the delinquent group which showed only one or two of the factors? Why weren't these youngsters among the non-delinquents?

These are only a few of the serious gaps in the investigation. As a basis for prediction the results would be dangerous if only on the ground that so many in the control group showed a greater incidence of the given factors than those in the delinquent group. Perhaps intensity of the factors, rather than their frequency, would provide better criteria for measuring delinquency potential.

The Ludden experiment, nevertheless, did bite off a little piece of a problem far too enormous for one investigator to chew.

That is, it demonstrated that in a certain city, among certain children, a certain set of easily ascertainable factors was prone to characterize 69 percent of known delinquents —as well as 25 percent of non-delinquents.

Fine, you may say. But what of it? Anybody in his right mind must know that a kid who plays truant, gets left back in school, is pretty stupid, and comes from an impoverished or broken home, may be more liable than others to turn out "bad" and get into trouble with the authorities.

You don't need expensive experiments in order to establish that!

Not so . . . nothing of the sort is definitely established anywhere. . . .

Remember that in the Ludden investigation, as in numerous others, the only overt distinction placing a boy in the "delinquent" group was that he had been picked up one or more times by the police. Doubtless in the control group there were many quite as delinquent—except that they had escaped police attention. This could explain the high incidence of "delinquency" factors among the control boys and girls.

Also, the lad who is intelligent, though he be delinquent, tends to have better success at avoiding the attention of the police; he may know enough to cover his tracks and hide his transgressions, to get others to do his dirty work for him. Further, his very intelligence, perhaps, makes him more amenable to school, so that as a result he is less frequently tardy or absent and manages to squeak by in his studies—though he may not be any the less delinquent on that account.

As for such factors as impoverished homes and living in a slum area, delinquency occasionally rears its ugly head even higher in our best neighborhoods than in the districts across the tracks. The only thing is, delinquency in garden spots takes a form different from that in slum sections—is more often concerned with sex and sensation than stealing and gangsterism. In high schools of plush Long Island, Westchester, Union County (N. J.) and other suburban areas around New York, for instance, kids who would not think of stealing are far less inhibited about rolling each other in the hay. This holds true, child experts and local school principals know, in the well-off suburban areas which surround Los Angeles, Chicago and most other large cities. Here the orgies, seductions, homosexual adventures and drinking parties—not to mention pregnancies—which occur among teen-agers rarely make the papers or engage the attention of the police. Why? Because prosperous parents can afford to protect their children. They call in a psychoanalyst rather than a case worker, or they simply get their straying daughters quietly aborted and keep silent; anything to avoid scandal.

The more intelligent or more privileged youngster, then, is not necessarily the less delinquent one; he may be simply the one more likely to stay out of the hands of the courts and police.

Here we see the danger of approaching the juvenile delinquency puzzle with any preconceived or fixed notions. Nothing can be taken for granted about this jigsaw, not even "what everybody knows"—to wit, that truant, low-intelligence, slum lads are more predisposed to errant behavior than their more fortunate brethren. Everything remains to be proved—or disproved—by exactly such investigations as the Ludden one.

This holds true not only for lay, popular conceptions about delinquency, such as "Jimmy steals because his father is no good." It equally applies to some of the most treasured and widely accepted shibboleths among professionals in the field, like the analysis-trained social worker's "Jimmy steals because of his insecurity."

Many Jimmies whose fathers are no good—and who are pathologically insecure in their feelings—nevertheless do not steal.

Plainly, the common factor of juvenile stealing, if one exists, must reside elsewhere.

It is only fair to admit that most youth workers fully realize there is no pat or simple explanation of delinquency. But in attempting to generalize methods of attack and cure, they may fall into the error of riding one horse too often, and up a one-way street—the color of the horse, of course, depending on whether their supervising authority is a Freudian analyst, clinical psychologist, penal expert or just some local politician.

Many studies before and since have probed delinquency along the lines of the Ludden attempt. Often they have gone much more deeply and exhaustively into the subject, using more extensively the methods of factorial analysis to get at causes and predisposing factors through information available in schools. Such surveys, while numerically frequent, are nevertheless far too few in proportion to the enormity and importance of the problem, and should be encouraged by civic support. For on a thousand Main Streets and Broadways they are gradually delimiting the aura of mystery, and the area of the unknown, surrounding this thing called delinquency.

It so happens, for example, that another valuable study was being completed in Passaic, New Jersey, at about the same time that Ludden was conducting his. W. C.

Kvaraceus, a top school official, produced figures covering a five-year period which tended to support Ludden's findings —at least in the matter of under-intelligence and low scholastic status being to a certain extent associated with delinquency.

Thus, among 563 delinquent boys and 198 girls, the mean I.Q. was discovered to be 89—compared to a score of 103 for the general school population.

Furthermore, 44 percent of the delinquent group had been retarded at least one term, whereas but 17 percent of the general group had been thus retarded. And the Passaic research turned up one really startling figure: no less than 29 percent of the delinquents had failed three terms or more, a record matched by a tiny one-half of one percent of the general population!

So far, so good. But this investigation was out to prove a point. Mr. Kvaraceus believed, with Dollard and other authorities, that frustration in the human animal *always* leads to aggression—and that aggression is *always* a product of frustration.

He further believed that the common crimes of youth— stealing, damaging property, indulging in aberrant sex practices, fleeing from home, playing truant and the like—were often simply expressions of this "aggression." It followed that "a search for causes or predisposing factors of delinquency should be a search for situations that frustrate." And he thought that his figures indicated such a situation in the schools.

In other words, education itself was at fault.

It made delinquents out of slow children by giving them curriculums too tough for them to handle—which frustrated them—which made them aggressive—which caused them to run away from home or steal cars.

Now there is considerable plausibility in this logic. But we have already seen that the vigorous personality trait can cut both ways. Aggression makes one boy a gang leader— and another a successful prize-fighter. And suppose we grant for argument's sake that the over-frustrated child becomes **over-aggressive and therefore** inclined to get himself into trouble. This might be nature's own method of recompense, of maintaining equilibrium in the survival mechanism. Would we, perhaps, by tampering with frustrating factors and thus killing aggressive tendencies, be preventing the rise of mobsters, yes—but also of sports heroes, generals and others requiring large muscles in the aggression department?

Besides, in its zeal the Passaic investigation placed the cart a little before that pet horse! Is aggression more a factor in juvenile stealing than, say, want and poverty? Does the aggressive kid damage property more often than the one too lacking in aggressiveness to avenge himself in any other way on a society he believes unjust?

Is it possible that truancy sometimes betokens simple fear, social timidity or the like, rather than large bumps of aggressiveness?

Fortunately, Kvaraceus did not jockey his pony into a pocket on the assumption that his lane was the only winning one.

Careful sifting of the figures and factorial analysis forced him to the mild conclusion that "aggression" could at best account for only certain manifestations of delinquency, and for even those merely in part.

For this conclusion alone the Passaic probe was valuable. Yet whole regiments in the anti-delinquency army failed to heed its lesson, and that of numerous experiments like it . . . which leads us to again stress the need for the alert eye, the elastic outlook, in fighting child crime.

To appreciate this, one must realize that the delinquency factors emphasized among experts, like educational methods, run in cycles. What was stylish last year is out of fashion today, though in time, as with short skirts, it may return to popularity.

Thus, a few years back, a causative factor generally à la mode was "revolt." This causative factor was replaced by "insecurity."

Then the latter became rather "old hat" and yielded, not without a struggle, to that same "aggression" which preoccupied Passaic.

So it may be of interest to note that New York City—the sheer bulk of whose delinquency problem has given it fruitful experience in these matters—recently circulated a new instruction to teachers. They were advised to concentrate no longer on "aggressive" children as candidates for entire schools the city devotes to those deemed predisposed to delinquency.

Nor were such types to be favored for remedial treatment by the city's Child Guidance Bureau.

The aggressive youngster, the authorities had come to believe, generally could manage to get along, to come to terms with life somehow.

It was actually the withheld, withdrawn child who was more likely to become maladjusted—and a really serious delinquent.

Truth in this view? Quite possibly. No doubt it will become very stylish.

One reason for mentioning the Passaic study is that it differed from others of the sort in one important sense. It took a critical attitude toward the schools themselves. It considered them possible accomplices of the delinquent, or, at least, accessories before the fact.

If the schools were spawning frustrated young characters, ran the argument, they had a direct share in predisposing for delinquency.

Well, the results showed that even where frustration, by inducing aggressive tendencies, might be responsible for some misbehavior, that same frustration did not arise solely from factors in the school.

As we might suspect, it derived as well from inherent and acquired personality quirks, and from the general or home environment.

The study concluded that just as no single factor could be demonstrated to be at fault for delinquency, so no single institution or agency could hope to cope with it—even the school.

But the studies raised important issues! The exact effects

of the school on juvenile behavior, for better or worse, have never been exhaustively examined. The whole amorphous relationship of the school to the delinquency problem is little understood.

"Frustrating" factors in the classroom are only one aspect of the delinquency complex; are there others more important?

Can the schools, indeed, be responsible for a good share of delinquency—hard as this might be for our educators to swallow?

Let us see.

13

Whose Blame?

WE ARE FUMBLING WITH JUVENILE DELINQUENCY BE-
cause everybody is blaming everybody else—parents blame
the schools; schools blame the parents and the courts. We
all blame the movie industry. No progress can be made until
each institution concerned with young people takes stock
of its own relationships to the problem and considers what
improvements can be made." She has something there, does
Counselor Faust of the Philadelphia schools.

So let us do a little stock-taking.

THE SCHOOLS

We start, with Miss Faust, in education. Reporting in the
Forum on studies completed in 1947, she reaches the same
conclusion which has struck so many others. "The schools
are in a strategic position to locate potential delinquency"
—and to do something about it.

Some go even further. Harry D. Gideonse, president of
Brooklyn College, speaks for them when he says: "The *only*
social agency to solve the problem is the school—because it
is the only one which touches all children."

That's putting it a little strongly. The school may reach
all children—but many agencies reach *some* children. Together they achieve considerable coverage and may be in a
position to make important contributions. Still, this does
not change the fact that when the home falls short, the
school appears by far the most practical instrument to detect shortcomings in the child and remedy them.

Yet delinquency exists. So the school to some extent must
be falling down on the job. Or better; is not adequately un-
dertaking it.

Could it be that school people do not believe delinquency

properly their responsibility? Should it be left to welfare departments and police, to community councils?

The reply could be that since the school is in a position to render invaluable help, this alone puts it under obligation to do so. "Those that can, must"—just as a doctor "must" help the sick.

But a more direct consideration is that the school's whole task—the work for which teachers draw pay (such as it is) —consists in training children for social living. *Therefore, to the extent that a child is asocial, the school has failed.* No use arguing that the origins of the maladjustment may lie beyond the school's control—in the child's home, his economic environment, his physical handicaps. The origins of a fever may lie beyond the doctor's control—but if the patient dies, the doctor fails, the profession of medicine fails.

So delinquency, being prominent among asocial phenomena, is correctly enough a school responsibility. And the schools by and large do not shirk it. Professionally as a group, individually as human beings, teachers are quick enough to recognize their function in plugging the dike. In surprisingly many communities they are the only ones who do anything at all about systematically preventing delinquency—this in a quiet unsung way, year in and year out, doing the best they can with each behavior problem as it comes up in the classroom.

If the school, then, in part fails, it is not for any fundamental want of conscientiousness. Let us look at the supposed advantages of the school as a delinquency-stopper, to see whether the trouble lies there:

1. *It is said that the school alone competes with the home in point of number of children reached and time spent with each child.*

Clearly true. Occasionally a well-meant curricular digression may result in truancy, as in the case of the "released time" program in New York City. By this arrangement, if the parents so desire, children may take off a certain number of school hours to go to church schools for religious instruction. In practice, a considerable number take off the hours—but spend the time in the streets. Right now the program is evoking hearty opposition on many grounds from educators, but continues under the pressure of religious hierarchies.

The writer, however, is not one of those who holds that a very occasional day off from school is necessarily bad; it may do a boy's soul a lot of good, particularly if the Giants are playing the Dodgers. It is only pernicious and symptomatic truancy which holds danger. And this is encountered to any great extent chiefly in rural districts, where children may be encouraged to stay at home for chores and field work at certain seasons. Certain parents "do not see the sense of schooling," and encourage truancy on general grounds. Also, in many agricultural districts, the school season may be too short at best, so that even minor truancy becomes seriously damaging.

In these rural areas, the extent of truancy interferes appreciably with the "school reaching every child." Yet in a great majority of rural counties no specific person exists to enforce the attendance laws! Principals and teachers in stubborn cases must go to the courts, a time-consuming, wasteful process—and often unsuccessful, believe it or not, because the rural magistrate may be in sympathy with the accused parents!

2. *It is claimed that the school is in an ideal position to develop data on every child and his community environment.*

Likewise true. Except for one thing. Teachers are already burdened with more bookkeeping than they have time for, not to mention marking tests and grading papers. It is quite conceivable that teachers and principals can be trained as psychometrists; and many are. But if they concentrate on measuring and compiling, other phases of schoolwork must suffer neglect.

Keeping statistics is a full-time job in any system of more than a thousand pupils, more than forty classrooms. Health and other vital statistics make a fair showing in most school systems, but only one child in ten attends a school where psychometric information is reasonably complete or even reasonably accurate. Only when systems hire and assign

more specialists will data proceed to become "full." Until
that day a certain number of behavior problems must go
unnoticed and untended until beyond the incipient stage.
Worse, behavior problems will be created in the classroom
itself, through inadequate knowledge of the child's traits
and background.

3. *Only the schools have a large reservoir of people em-
pirically and academically prepared to deal with children.*

No dispute. But the classroom teacher is already carrying
as heavy a burden as possible. At most she can be expected
to be a teacher, not a specialist in behavior problems. Yet
all kinds of delinquency programs are emanating constantly
from all kinds of authorities, obliging the teacher to do this
for "aggressive" pupils, that for "disturbed" ones—to maintain intricate contacts with disturbed pupils' parents—to
run therapeutic "clubs" and group projects after school
hours—and to do Lord knows how many other things, as if
all her pupils were delinquents and she a clinic. All at no ex-
tra pay, of course.

The teacher's function in the delinquency set-up should
be to locate behavior abnormalities and alleviate them if
she can—and if alleviation does not mean neglect of her
other pupils. But if the individual problem begins to take
up too much classroom time, or if it persists, grows out of
hand, she should have specialists available to whom to refer
that problem.

Of course, virtually every school system today does have
some place of ultimate referral. In one school out of two it
is the police, a county court officer or a magistrate. In many
larger systems it is a special class or school for "problem"
children. But only a handful have anything even approaching New York City's Child Guidance Bureau, at which
psychiatric, case and group work and other therapies are
available. And even this exemplary school bureau is so un-
derstaffed that one psychiatric case worker, entrusted with
twelve schools including a high school, told the writer that
during a whole school year she had managed to visit only
five of them!

No need to go further down the list. While the school

has many counter-delinquency potentialities, obviously each is being realized only in a limited way. Qualified personnel are essential; yet average teacher pay is less than $50 weekly, states the National Education Association. Other abuses spring from the political nature of many school appointments, with principals and supervisors being selected for political reasons rather than fitness. Under such supervision, and often enough underpaid and overburdened, the teacher may become a behavior problem herself; certainly her capacity to help children suffers.

But such flaws cannot be blamed on the school. They arise from our own complacency, and our stinginess. By and large, Federal investigation has shown, people get the kind of schools they want and pay for. So let each of us in our various communities—especially the parents among us—quit bewailing the faults of dear Tommy's teacher and demanding the impossible of her. It's time we either put up or shut up.

Not that this is intended to whitewash the school's part in creating delinquents! Any "stock-taking" must reveal ample room for school self-improvement even under existing conditions.

The fixing of qualifications, for one thing, at present is arbitrary and confused. In the effort to get people of high standard, most boards of education emphasize academic training. They incline to forget what the Social Service Division puts this way: "The teacher one recalls from his own childhood is not necessarily the one who knew the most history or mathematics, but the one who was most responsive to children and stimulated them most to widen their horizons."

In several cases known to the writer, teachers of really superb ability have been refused permanent appointment or offered lower salary scales because they lacked a few college credits—although they were graduates of accepted state normal schools. In another representative instance, a woman of twenty years' highly successful experience in an excellent municipal school system moved to New York, qualified as a substitute, and was given seventeen behavior problems in a slum district to handle in one class. This she did with such success that the Child Guidance Bureau itself commended her, and parents in the troubled, underprivileged neighborhood got up a petition of thanks. Her principal described her as "indispensable to our school and neighborhood." She took the regular-teacher examination that term, passed twelfth out of 2000—and was turned down for appointment because she was a few months over the varying age limitation, which happened to be set at forty years just before she took the examination!

Boards of education are merely begging the question by choosing teachers on the basis of arbitrary requirements. Each teacher should be considered separately on her merits —eligibility to depend on fitness and capacity, and nothing else.

Another criticism, as summarized in the Federal panel report, *School and Teacher Responsibilities,* is that: "Too few systems have met the problem of education for religious and racial minority groups. Conflict arises out of this area of strain and is a common cause of individual and group delinquency."

In one notorious slum trouble-spot, a grade and junior high school functioning in the same enormous building, the desperate principals hit on this expedient. Spanish-speaking kids, many of them in the country two or three years or less, were directed to entertain in the assembly with their native songs and dances—in this case, chiefly rhumbas. Similarly, each week Negro students showed what they could do in the way of tap-dancing and spirituals. Holidays were celebrated in this fashion: Jewish children participated in Christmas and Easter pageants, which is common, and Gentile children, including Negroes, participated in Chanukah plays, which is not. The Spanish-speaking kids put on an Easter fiesta of their own, with exotic native ritual and music—but only after laboriously coaching the rest of the school population to participate. *Each group suddenly learned about the other, gaining respect and fellowship.* True, one grateful lad stole a string of beads from a variety store to present to his teacher at Christmas time. But the number of delinquent acts participated in by kids in the school decreased eighty-seven percent in ten months! The police precinct captain personally called on the two principals to thank them.

This is all part of the democratization process entrusted to the schools by America's founding fathers—a trust which sometimes teachers forget. Too often they hold obedience above self-expression, conformance above initiative. Too often, though today teachers certainly know better, subject matter remains the thing rather than the individual child himself.

And in most cities the best teachers, like the best equipment, are assigned to wealthier neighborhoods where classes are least crowded and child adjustment least difficult. Often teachers preserve prejudices themselves, regarding it as a punishment or slight to be sent to difficult schools, slum schools, schools with the minority-group children who may need skilled help most.

So before the school can fully rise to the problem of delinquency it needs certain overhauling within and certain support from without. Notably, financial support. Perhaps we could do with a few highways and atom bombs less. Children are every bit as important to the future of the nation.

THE HOME

Each year hundreds of thousands of juveniles get into slight or serious trouble. Each year many millions of juveniles do not!

The law-abiding kids may be full of spit and vinegar, bursting with mischief; or they may be shy and quiet. Some are placid, some excitable. Even the happy ones have troubles of their own. But these are the fortunate children . . . Their homes give them the security, the training in ways of life, the resources and fortitudes, which are essential to social living! For the home is the keystone of communal organization, and when it falls the whole complex structure falls. It is the crucible in which character and personality are formed. It is here that the twig is bent, that the child sucks in social attitudes with his mother's milk—or the pediatrician's formula. Only when the home falters does the school, the welfare agency, the probation officer, have to take over; that, at least, is the most widely accepted theory among delinquency experts at the moment.

We may accept as clearly valid that homes broken by death or divorce—and at present one marriage in three is headed for the divorce court!—are found in association with numbers of delinquency and neglect cases. So is the home upset by mental or physical illness, uprooted in the pursuit of employment or living space, beset by poverty, or otherwise disturbed by the strains of modern civilized life.

To attack delinquency at the source, then, home help would appear essential. Minimum financial relief in time of emergency is now pretty well accepted as a community obligation. But other types of relief are not. The home in disturbance needs counsel, guidance and often mental hygiene of sorts. Sometimes these are available from church groups in the community, sometimes from public agencies. But welfare systems all over the country are scattered, uneven, poorly manned, working on low rather than optimum budgets, and in many sections, particularly rural ones, not available at all.

But homes technically "broken" in one way or another are found in association with only some 20 to 30 percent of delinquency cases coming before the courts. The rest stem from homes which on the face of things are holding together, yet somehow fail to meet the needs of their young ones.

For this, mothers and fathers are coming in for vitriolic criticism. It has now become a popular sport of schools, police departments and courts, not to mention our famous F.B.I. head, to blame parents for delinquency. Discouraged by a constant procession of juvenile burglars, car stealers, unwed mothers and armed members of street gangs, magistrates like New York's Charles E. Ramsgate understandably grow bitter against lack of home supervision. "Today parents rely on schools and churches to teach respect for others which is the basis of decent society. It's their own primary obligation!"

On this theory, a considerable number of judges have

been sentencing "delinquent" parents. Nationally syndicated columnists vigorously support the idea. The National Council of Juvenile Court Judges heard a declaration to the effect that ". . . 85 percent of juvenile delinquency is the result of inadequate upbringing. Parents should be made subject to court action in all parts of the country."

Well, is there hope in this direction? Can parents be shocked, pounded or threatened into taking better care of their children?

We need not guess at the answer. It happens that a proving-ground exists in Toledo, Ohio, which has been punishing delinquent parents for more than ten years.

And after a comprehensive survey of results in the 1937-1946 interval, Judge Paul W. Alexander of the Toledo (Lucas County) Juvenile Court published these conclusions in *Federal Probation:* (a) As a method of curbing delinquency, parent punishment fails—for the delinquency rate continued to rise despite more and more punishments. (b) As a method of reforming guilty parents and frightening others into behaving themselves, it also fails. (c) As a method of defending society, imprisonment is indefensible legally, since the parents' threat is not "immediate or direct," except against their own children. (d) As a method of vengeance, punishment works excellently, satisfying the "punitive-vindicative appetite of self-righteous nondelinquent parents and irritated public authorities . . ."

The Alexander findings indicated that in certain select cases, where other methods fail, prosecution and *threat* of punishment—not actual punishment—could do some good. But he reminds us:

It is generally impossible to punish the parent without at the same time punishing the child. Imprisonment usually means breaking up the family. Fines mean depriving the child and family of so much sustenance. What most parents of delinquent or neglected children need is help.

A similar conclusion was reached in a parallel investigation by Samuel Whiteman, director of the Cleveland Mental

Hygiene Association. He points out that parents' insufficiencies generally trace to those of their own parents. With respect to those who would punish or "blame," he says: "The most serious fallacy in the thinking of these zealous critics lies in the assumption that parents are aware of their own shortcomings and deliberately plan to misguide and mistreat children. From the cases seen in child guidance clinics, it has been observed that parental guidance contributing to a child's poor adjustment is largely unintentional and unwitting."

The fact is that most of America's millions of parents are doing their level best to bring up their children as good citizens. But sometimes, being human, they go a little off course due to ignorance—or lack of means—or mishaps such as sickness—or perhaps deficiencies in their own personalities.

To blame them for such things is both foolish and useless. "Delinquent" parents are like delinquent juveniles; they require not criticism, but teaching and help.

Every parent, however, may profitably "take stock." If you are a mother or father, and you find your child maladjusted or misbehaved, look to yourself; don't try to blame his teachers, the movies or "this lousy neighborhood." Ask yourself if you are giving the kid, at the very least, these essentials:

1. The *affection* he deserves as your child.
2. The *respect, confidence and consideration* he deserves as a person.
3. A feeling of *security* through your own steadfast loyalty to him, and, if you can manage it, your fortitude in the face of difficulties.
4. Sufficient of your *time and companionship,* when he wants them.
5. The participation in *family planning* and affairs necessary to his self-respect, and essential to train him for living in a democratic society.
6. *Emotional stability* which results from your own calmness, humor and consistent attitudes toward him, your

control of moods and temper—and your even, pleasant relationships with other members of the family.

7. A *tolerant view* toward persons of all cultures and colors, of high and low degree—given him through lessons learned at your knee, and through your own toleration of his reasonable wishes or beliefs.

8. The *courtesy* of seeking expert assistance if despite yourself you find the child disturbed or straying.

Quite a recipe? It still lacks an ingredient. Add a bit of seasoning in the way of restrained but firm discipline when you deem it necessary.

POLICE AND COURTS

Any police officer worth his salt knows, or should know, that the rights and welfare of the individual are of paramount importance in the American way of life. He is sworn to uphold such rights. Yet he has a higher loyalty; he must defend the community against marauders.

When the individual violates rules set up in the general interest, the policeman has no choice but to curtail that individual's liberty.

Nevertheless, his duty to the individual remains, insofar as it does not conflict with his duty to the community. Besides—attention to individual welfare comes under the head of good, practical police work! "The delinquent of today is the serious criminal of tomorrow"—so police and penal records tell us.

Thus, it has come to be recognized that helping kids in trouble is as important a police function as that of arresting them.

In several ways, the police officer stands in a unique position to forestall delinquency and curtail it when it does appear. In the first place, he is the initial official contact between children in trouble—or on the verge of trouble—and the austere law. "The manner in which the officer handles the child in his first difficulty may be the making or breaking of the youngster's future life," warns an authoritative manual on delinquency compiled by the National

Advisory Police Committee. A companion manual for policewomen states: "First contact with the police is like first aid treatment . . . the individual's chances for recovery largely depend on the handling he receives during that critical experience. Many a gang has been welded together by a common hatred for police, born of some unfortunate experience with unskilled officers."

In "taking stock," therefore, law-enforcement personnel should ask themselves whether the officer on the beat conducts himself to advantage. He can be a great force for good by acting with firmness, yes—but with understanding and generosity as well. Most first offenses are relatively minor and may be treated with warnings rather than arrests. But the officer should use the occasion to win the confidence and respect of the offender if he can; to guide, explain and correct rather than chide.

Even on second offenses, further efforts with the child and a tactful visit or two to his parents often serve as sufficient corrective.

Alert police officers have frequently noticed that simple friendliness in itself may be enough to help juveniles who err because they are discouraged, or feel unaccepted by society.

On the other hand, unfriendly, curt and arbitrary methods can only further accentuate the anti-social attitudes of any youngster.

A second prime responsibility arises from the fact that the police are best qualified to protect juveniles from certain harmful community influences. The police best know the trouble areas, the sources of infection, the centers of temptation and vice. It is they who can observe dancehall and bar, keep watch for panderer and pervert. It is they who have the direct authority and "know-how" to deal with irregularities.

Emotionally stable and adequately informed kids can themselves repel evil influence in most cases. Less fortunate children may find themselves victimized, lured and seduced into the ways of delinquency unless the policeman stands between them and adult exploitation.

Finally, police departments themselves have come to the realization that juvenile problems can best be handled by a separate branch—operating in many communities today under such titles as *juvenile police* or *juvenile bureau*. Such a bureau is especially effective on the preventative side, since it facilitates liason with other community groups concerned with the problem—schools, churches, child clinics and welfare agencies. Thousands of cases are disposed of without the necessity of dragging the offender into court and labeling him "delinquent." Thousands of near-delinquents are diverted to corrective agencies before they can get themselves into real trouble.

Admittedly, police work in this country leaves much to be desired. Yet it seems to this writer that within their limits the police are doing a rather good job with children. Constant experience with all types of offenders apparently arms the corner cop with patience, resource and a kind of practical good sense often invaluable in dealing with youthful offenders.

Still, while all behavior problems are not delinquencies, all delinquencies are behavior problems. To deal with them adequately requires special skills—and a certain amount of research. Here, if anywhere, police departments show a major lack.

However, a start has been made in several states both at training the police officer for delinquency control and conducting research into methods of such control.

One notable experiment along these lines is being conducted at the University of Southern California under the sponsorship of various law-enforcement agencies of the state. There, experts in all fields of child behavior conduct investigations and give concentrated training to selected police officers from various municipal, county and state departments. Officers from other states are also encouraged to attend. Professor Norris E. Class, affiliated with the school, points out that it may not be the best answer to training staff members for juvenile bureaus. "Many different approaches to such training have to be made—and the best of each welded into a new 'best' approach." Meanwhile the

California school is functioning as an excellent training facility—one which could be copied to advantage in other parts of the country.

When the police bring in a young offender whose case warrants judicial action, it goes to a special court based on the idea that an erring child deserves correction and help rather than punishment. These "juvenile courts" are available in every state, with jurisdiction over offending or neglected children up to 18 years of age, sometimes up to 16 years.

Often they function as parts of other courts, or through special children's procedures within the latter.

Magistrates in such courts have an exceedingly difficult task. Not only must they know the law and enforce it; they must know—and like—children. Theirs is the responsibility of deciding whether the child goes to reform school or foster home—whether he can be helped by "another chance"—whether he should be referred to welfare agencies—whether "probation officers" will be able to cope with the case.

On the whole, the quality of justice in juvenile courts can give rise to no major complaint, except that politics often dictates the choice of judges. Even so, by and large the children's magistrate performs intelligently, diligently and with conscience.

But a "stock-taking" reveals several serious deficiencies in the juvenile court set-up. To be successful in correcting the wayward juvenile, the judge requires expert technical assistance, and, above all, ample referral facilities. In communities where these exist and cooperate with the court, fine and dandy. Sometimes they are even part of the court, which has its own complete staff of medical, psychiatric and other experts, working through a child clinic. On the other hand, all too many courts have only the services of probation officers to depend on.

Standards in all these respects have been developed and promulgated by the Children's Bureau, the National Probation Association, and the White House Conferences on Child Care and Protection. Now, more than twenty-five years after they were first codified, the country still lags sadly behind those standards.

Take probation work, on which the court must rely so heavily. Obviously the probation officer should be a highly trained, exeptionally capable social worker—and so he is, except in many rural sections and urban ones too, where he is appointed on the strength of whom he knows rather than what he knows! As a group, probation officers are probably the most underpaid of all public servants, and among the most overburdened. Also, occasionally there arises a kind of tug-of-war between judges whose outlook is more or less legalistic and probation officers concerned more with reclamation than justice. Such judges allow little room for application of the officer's special abilities, viewing the latter as a sort of policeman. In fact, Warrington Stokes of the Portland (Ore.) Public Welfare Commission told the 1947 National Conference of Social Work that "many judges have a tendency to treat the social workers as little more than glorified errand boys."

Perhaps there is truth, then, in what Dr. Thomas D. Elliot of the National Probation Association first argued in 1937, thus summarized by Alice Scott Nutt of the Federal Child Guidance Division: "Essentially judicial functions are incongruous with functions of child care and treatment. When incongruous functions are performed by a single agency, social efficiency is retarded and motivations and attitudes clouded."

And certainly there is truth in the contention that confused jurisdictions, jumbled standards and uneven facilities plague the work of the juvenile courts.

Accordingly, a growing trend is in evidence to remove all corrective functions from the court and have it stick to legal ones only. Either it could refer all correction to an officially designated agency, or, as in New York, such an agency could first pass on all delinquency cases, and itself decide which particular cases should be referred to the court for legal action.

This is far from the only way out, in the author's belief. Courts, like the police, are advantageously placed by experience and authority to deal with delinquency as criminality, as threat against society.

But no court can overcome the handicap of insufficient corollary services! Should communities make these sufficiently available at the court's discretion, judges will be better able to temper justice not merely with mercy, but with cure and prevention.

SOCIAL SERVICES

One service of particular value to the court, for example, is the child guidance "clinic" utilizing the skills of psychiatrist, psychologist and psychiatric social worker. A few courts boast such clinics under their own auspices. They are available in some communities as adjuncts of the school, hospitals or welfare agencies. But nearly half of America's juvenile courts, and more than half of America's children, must do without the diagnostic and therapeutic services such clinics provide.

Similarly, other social services are sometimes available for disturbed children, sometimes not. To control a social phenomenon as complex as juvenile delinquency, a many-sided attack is needed. A school, for instance, cannot help little Tommy much if every time he goes home his drunken father gives him a beating and his mother is busy entertaining customers in the bedroom. In such a hypothetical case, various social services would be obliged to step in and lend a hand.

A state welfare department, for example, could pay the rent and relieve Tommy's mother of her financial strain. An employment bureau could then find his father a job—after a neighborhood church family-welfare agency had helped him cure himself of drinking. A public health clinic could cure him of the vitamin deficiency caused by alcohol. A family-service mental hygienist might rid him of his habit of beating Tommy. Such sources of assistance come under the designation of "social service." They include settlement houses, parent education classes, recreational facilities, aids to dependent or ill children, vocational guidance, nursing care, visiting teachers and other specialized types of help in almost endless variety They may be furnished by public welfare agencies under municipal, county or state auspices —or by private groups, foundations and churches. But in hundreds of cities and rural counties they are available too little and too late—or not at all.

This appalling condition is customarily blamed on state welfare departments, whose function it is to see that a sufficiency of child-welfare services are available from either public or private sources.

The blame, of course, is not theirs but ours.

When each of us, within our means, gives sufficient money, support and participation, then will our public agencies and private ones be able to furnish what the Department of Labor calls for in its recommended program for controlling juvenile delinquency:

> Social services adapted to the needs of any child who presents behavior problems in the home, school or elsewhere, and made available to parents, teachers, police, court officials and others who deal with the child.

14

Whose Shame?

Our brief inventory is made. We have looked into the face of a problem that vitally affects the future of our country and our people. We have "taken stock" of social institutions, including the home, influencing the amount of delinquency, and of the direction of efforts to control it. But we still remain somewhat up in the air about basic causes. . . .

In previous chapters have been mentioned a few experimental approaches to the delinquency problem. These were chosen for what to the author seems both historical significance in showing the evolution of present thinking on the subject—and illustrative value in showing some trends pursued by later researches. Many of these far exceed in scope and importance such individual investigations as those of Kvaraceus, or group efforts like the Judge Baker Guidance Clinic; a scant few even match the pioneering contributions of New York's Child Guidance Bureau, the California Youth Authority and the St. Paul experiment.

Among the most productive of the various research projects must be classed a memorable investigation by Connecticut authorities in 1946-47.

It stands as a milestone in the long hunt for "causes" of child crime.

Connecticut's Public Welfare Commission felt, perhaps rather optimistically, that it knew pretty well how to best handle a child *after* he had become delinquent. The trouble was that two out of every hundred children in the state were requiring such handling, on grounds of waywardness or neglect. With both the child population and the delinquency trend going up, costs were enormous! The Commission decided to try on its own hook to slay the dragon of basic causes, if only to "reduce the number of children need-ing long-time expensive care."

Enlisting the technical services of Community Surveys Inc., under Reginald Robinson, the Commission authorized a thorough breakdown of all material facts about 4,035 families responsible for 4,788 delinquent or neglected children in 1945. Next, from these an arithmetical sample of 378 families was chosen and subjected to case-by-case inspection. Finally, a special analysis was made of families in Stamford, aligning with the over-all picture the various social statistics from that city.

Without going further into the methodology, it may be stated that this was the first exhaustive, scientific attempt on a state-wide basis to peer beneath the surface of delinquency. As might be expected, some of its findings proved startling! It substantiated what a number of researchers were beginning to suspect and a few in a small way had attempted to demonstrate:

1. So far as getting at causes is concerned, study of external traits such as age, sex, religion, economic status, size of family, place of residence and the like—all "lead up blind alleys."

2. The proportion of foreign-born fathers of delinquent children is almost exactly the same as the proportion of foreign-born males over 25 in the general population. Thus end attempts to pin delinquency on the nativity of parents.

3. The proportion of non-white delinquents is not significantly greater than that of white delinquents. But there are *exactly* the same number of non-white delinquent children—and non-white neglected children!

4. Popularly blamed "causes" such as broken homes, large families, low income, and poor housing in themselves do not create delinquency.

5. In Connecticut, at least, community or neighborhood environment shows no important causal effect on delinquency. The state has no huge, crowded cities of the type where child crime runs wild in "delinquency areas." Yet its rate of delinquency continues high.

6. Delinquency persists despite one of the best child wel-

fare records in the Union, dating back to 1921! Child social services and recreational facilities, public and private, as well as juvenile court, probation and training systems, far surpass those of most other states; so the "blame" for delinquency would seem to lie elsewhere.

For these findings alone, the survey would have been invaluable. As previously remarked, all researches into causes and controls should be encouraged, if only to narrow the field of search.

Unfortunately, proceeding from this point, the Connecticut investigators made something of a mistake. The author feels that they were justified on all the evidence to assume that delinquency, as a behavior problem, is merely a symptom of other disturbances. But they were not justified, in a scientific sense, in assuming that the other disturbances were necessarily family ones. Why not disturbances in the church? The political situation? The endocrine balance? Why not disturbances due, for the sake of argument, to over-zealous psychiatrists and teachers and state welfare departments tampering too much, or in false directions, with children's early adjustments?

The Connecticut survey missed a golden opportunity to throw out all preconceived notions of what did or did not cause delinquency. Instead, having disproved a number of such notions, they proceeded on the theory that delinquency, like charity, begins at home.

A promising tack! Most police, welfare and court authities today agree that the seat of delinquency is somewhere in the home. Accordingly, statistically and by intensive case analysis, the survey sought evidences of family troubles wherever there were children's troubles. And again the investigation came up with some startling facts.

1. Of the arithmetical sample of 378 families, 57 consisted of neglect cases, 321 of delinquency cases. Among the latter, more than half showed possible symptoms of family breakdown such as crime, divorce, mental disease, mental deficiency, illegitimacy, economic need, ill health. In the writer's opinion, the startling thing is—*nearly half did not!*

2. Somewhat taken aback, the investigators sought other possible breakdown symptoms in fields which sometimes do not appear in official files, but which might make "unofficial" trouble: extra-marital sex relations, alcoholism, violent quarreling, separation, desertion, irregular work, non-support. Of all 378 families—including the neglect cases—217 showed one or more of these symptoms. *But 161 did not!*

3. In a separate control investigation into 1162 families in Stamford listed as showing the following irregularities—delinquency, neglect, crime, divorce, mental disease, mental deficiency—the Commission found that one-fourth of the families showing delinquency also showed symptoms in the other categories, assumed to indicate family breakdown. *But three out of four families did not!*

Despite these findings, the investigators kept boring into the family situation as the causal factor of delinquency. They took the view that if they *could* have gone deeply enough into the backgrounds of the families showing no breakdown symptoms, such symptoms in all probability *would* have turned up. They decided the figures confirmed the belief that delinquency has its roots in family disorganization.

Meanwhile they overlooked, or at least did not stress, some further startling information in their own mathematics, again importantly narrowing the field for future researchers.

Thus, the figures tended to show that while 63 percent of the neglect cases had a history of crime in the family—only 18 percent of the delinquency cases had such a history. Further, 46 percent of the neglect cases showed illegitimacy—but only 6 percent of the delinquency cases.

The largest single disturbance among the delinquent families was economic, with need occurring in 30 percent. Truancy as an actual delinquency occurred in 32 percent of these families.

But possibly the most suggestive statistic is this: Of all the neglect cases, one in three showed delinquency . . . so parental neglect may have something to do with causing it

Yet of all the delinquency cases, only one in ten showed neglect as a primary symptom! *Is it possible, despite the experts, that other things besides parental neglect can make a delinquent?*

Continuing its investigation into the type of delinquent which interested it, the one who came from a disorganized family, the survey came up with further shrewd and significant observations. It found, for example, that the *types* of disorganization in 281 of its 378 families ran about as follows: 56 percent, emotional instability; 10 percent, mental deficiency; 7 percent, disinterested parents; 5 percent, mental disease; 3 percent, ill health; 2 percent, incompatibility; 1 percent, cultural conflict (parents of different race or religion); .4 percent, economic need. The categories overlap, with families often showing more than one of these disturbances. Although economic need occurred in a considerable number of the families, for example, usually some other factor was more important in creating the disorganization. It should be noted that in 20 percent of these families, no identifying disturbance could be determined. Also, information on the missing 98 cases—mostly delinquency families—was too meager to be conclusive.

The survey further found that the family troubles, whatever they were, directly affected both delinquent and neglected children as follows: 32 percent, deprivation of affection; 28 percent, deprivation of family security; 18 percent, deprivation of physical necessities; 15 percent, deprivation of social opportunities; 12 percent, over-indulgence or over-protection; 4 percent, pressure from school or friends; 2 percent, exposure to (bad) neighborhood patterns. Again the categories overlap. And in 20 percent of these children, no definite effect of the family disturbance could be found.

From all this, the Connecticut people reached the conclusion that delinquency was chiefly caused by "family disorganization." It could therefore be best controlled by aiding families to avoid disorganization. The investigators made recommendations to that effect, calling for additional social services to families.

To repeat, a memorable investigation into delinquency, one of the most fruitful on record.

By far the most ambitious anti-delinquency project, however, was completed in 1946 by the National Conference on Prevention and Control of Juvenile Delinquency, called by Attorney General Tom C. Clark. This was not so much an experimental or research project as an exhaustive survey of all work in the field—all known facts, surmises and methods of approach—plus recommendations based on the sum of all experience to that date. Results were published in the form of eighteen separate reports, each covering a specific aspect of delinquency, each compiled by panels of dozens of leading experts.

One basic and underlying conclusion emerging from all the reports was that delinquency could not be fought on any single front. It could be conquered, if at all, only by extending and strengthening the whole complex of social services, making preventive and curative facilities available to all children—and social help available to all adults. The Connecticut survey, like many others, in the end came to a similar recommendation; it advised that not only child services, but family and parent services as well, be emphasized. These views are an inevitable outgrowth of what most delinquency experts finally begin to accept, thus expressed by the National Conference: "There are as many causes of delinquency as there are evils and errors in this world." And addressing itself to the American home, it warns:

> Nobody should be taken seriously who blames delinquency on "parents," on "cigarettes," on "mothers working," on "progressive education," on "the moving pictures," on "malnutrition" or on any other one cause. It does not matter who or what such a person is—how much he may know about something else. He is being careless or ignorant when he tries to "blame" anything as complicated as delinquency on any one thing.

The author thoroughly subscribes to this position. No

two kids are ever exactly the same, nor have exactly the same experiences. "Every delinquent act is a unique response to a unique situation." In view of such complexity, control can only occur through attack on all sides, from all social agencies, with all instruments available.

But one cannot help feeling that the work would be greatly speeded if only more were definitely established about causes. Not so foolish as he seems is one reform-school psychiatrist known to the author who is investigating a pet theory that delinquency often follows trauma during infancy—actual physical injury such as a fall on the head. Nor another investigator, a psychometrist, who has been struck by the high incidence of "Jr." attached to the names of maladjusted boys, and is looking for clues in that direction! Any common denominator of cause, no matter how slight, could foster a common ground of approach. A general direction, an orientation, a knowledge of just what they are trying to do, are lacking alike among parents and agencies manned by specialists. Says Dr. J. Franklin Robinson of the Wilkes-Barre Children's Service Center, commenting on trends in child guidance clinics: "We are on uncertain ground when we try to tell which (maladjusted) children will do poorly in later life. An evaluation at a given point cannot divine the future." For the sake of skilled psychiatrist and struggling mother, there should be no relaxation in the search for conditions predictably leading to delinquency. We know that causative conditions exist—for delinquency exists!

And already, as we have seen, the field has been greatly narrowed. There is legitimate hope for that surer indentification of the causes of delinquency which would prove so helpful.

The chief stumbling-block thus far is that too much remains to be explained away. Family breakdown may be a genuine cause of certain delinquencies. But as the Connecticut survey itself asks—what about the children in many disturbed families who do not become delinquent? What about two boys in the same disturbed family, one of whom becomes delinquent while the other does not?

We need nôt try to deny that in a white-hot slum area full of racial and economic tensions, delinquency lurks on every corner. Yet the great majority of children even there do not become delinquent! Why?

It would seem that no matter what the surrounding quicksands, it takes something to push the child into them. The broken homes, the poverties, the cultural tensions, the boredoms, none of these have fully demonstrated themselves the crucial factor—though they may be the material of the quicksands.

Yet from examination of thousands of cases, many of which have been mentioned in this book, the author has come to feel that a possible causative pattern makes itself visible. In the author's belief, if not the causes, then the categories of cause, must narrow to four:

First and most important—*lack of love!* Second—*lack of example!* Third—*lack of responsibilities!* And fourth—*lack of natural equipment!*

Of the first two, Katherine F. Lenroot, chief of the Children's Bureau, has said: "There are two things essential to childhood—love and example! Of these, the greater is love."

It is love, essentially, which gives a child the security and solidity to stand firm in the face of difficulty. Lack of it may lead to maladjustment in a variety of forms, including delinquency. Love, however, must be qualified—even mother love. It must be administered with wisdom. Over-indulgence and over-protection, let us remember, accounted for a good percentage of the delinquencies in Connecticut's disturbed families.

Over-solicitude on the part of parents may impart just as much delinquency potential on occasion as neglect. Conversely, it is the younger child in the large family, who, although relatively neglected by busy and aging parents, as often as not grows into a more solid citizen than his older brothers who enjoyed greater parental attention, if not devotion. And the only child, as everyone knows, being the sole object of warm, constant parental care, frequently is on that account rendered into a spoiled, maladjusted neurotic—the very prototype of the delinquent. It has even been said by certain sociologists that parents, being what they are, would often do better by their children to neglect them than to impose their own twisted codes, prejudices and superstitions on the defenseless youngsters.

However that may be, lack of warm yet balanced love, and of its overt evidences such as affection, are pretty well recognized as delinquency factors by most child authorities. Lack of good example—or conversely, abundance of unsound example—likewise are widely accepted as contributing factors. But the full implications of example seem scantily appreciated.

The National Advisory Police Committee's manual on delinquency, issued with the approval of the International Association of Chiefs of Police and the National Sheriff's Association, is one of the most practical and concise treatments of the subject. Among its many pithy remarks is one to the effect that its recommended techniques for delinquency prevention could very well serve for the prevention of prostitution. There is definite kinship between origins of prostitution and other sex crime, and origins of all delinquency. This became evident in an earlier chapter, when it was pointed out that the juvenile sex offense rises largely from the milieu. *Society fails to get its moral teachings across to the youngster because the adult does not live up to those teachings*. He falls short in example!

This he does, whether parent or teacher, whenever he loses his temper, is unjust, bullies. The parent who casually fibs over the telephone is making his child a liar. The mother who treats hired servants in some way to emphasize difference is creating an area of cultural tension. The elder brother who comes home with violent tales of war or love can expect a kid to try and follow in his footsteps. A child does not do as he is told. He does what he sees others do —chiefly those others he admires and loves. Even if all moral teachings and proscriptions were essentially false, so long as his elders followed them so would the child—at least until he grew up! For the child largely learns to handle himself by aping, by imitation, by patterning himself on those around him.

In some juvenile gang situations and other delinquencies, the offender is not behaving abnormally—but quite normally according to the actions of his circle. So far as the child can judge by what he observes, it is normal to make and carry a gun, normal to beat up the guys on the next block—just as it is normal for kids from shacks along the railroad to steal coal. All society must be on guard to impress on children by example that the proper thing is the normal thing.

And warns Dr. Brock Chisholm, United Nations social and child expert:

"The responsibility of parents and teachers of young children is to show in their own persons the kind of citizenship that will make it possible for the human race to survive in the future."

For the example that makes a delinquent is the example that can destroy a world.

Third comes the matter of giving children responsibility. This area has been singularly neglected by delinquency investigators. In all the hundreds of thousands of words of the National Conference on Prevention and Control, exhaustively reporting on the field, responsibility was mentioned only in two or three sentences—chiefly in the panel report on rural delinquency. There it was briefly observed that responsibilities given to children around farm homes seemed to inhibit delinquency.

Chores and home duties no longer fall to any great extent on the shoulders of city children. The Children's Bureau and other authorities recommend participation of kids in family planning and activities; this in part, perhaps, can serve as a substitute.

But putting duty and program upon a child cannot be neglected if delinquency is to be avoided. The writer's opinion is that responsibility is virtually as important to normal child growth as love—in fact it is a demonstration of the trust, need and acceptance which signify love. By responsibility is not meant any heavy tasks or weighty, complicated duties, or strict regimens of any kind. But just as a dog "goes bad" without a bit of work, so does a child. It is through responsibility that the youngster exercises his strengths, builds his character, acquires his self-discipline and control over his moods. If we love our children and fear for them, let us take the pains to see that each child has a service to perform, his and his only, according to his age and ability.

To neglect this is to neglect his growth!

Ask any probation officer or playground director how often giving responsiblity to an offending child has saved the day!

Such vesting of responsibility is an exhibition of trust, a sincere flattery. It heals the disturbed ego, and shapes the healthy one.

Most delinquencies in the end can be accounted for by the three mentioned lacks in the background of the child. But if he has these requisites and yet becomes delinquent, it could be because he is reacting abnormally because of faulty mental or physcal equipment. This is our fourth causal lack: lack of capacity to adjust because of mental deficiency, mental disease, physical handicaps, glandular disturbances. It is sickness. Often it can be cured by doctor or psychiatrist. If not, the child must be placed in a special environment at home or in an institution.

Otherwise the delinquent or quasi-delinquent child who is in this category must remain a menace to society and himself.

If we wish, we can look on it in this way—kids are born delinquent. As infants they are cute as puppies—and as animal as puppies. It is only the pressure of social restraint and moral teaching which gradually confines the beast; and these are transmitted, if the child has healthy responses, by love—by example—by the taste of responsibility. Without these three pressures, nothing exists to confine the savage, to convert him into a social creature.

So let us all, in homes or in bureaus, try to see that every child gets warm affection and acceptance. Let us set the example for tomorrow by our example today—in the conduct of our businesses, our persons, our lives. Let us give every child a game, and a task as well. All play and no work may make Jack a delinquent boy.

And to keep our powder dry, let us extend and improve all institutions, schools and services dealing with children directly or through their families—not only disturbed children, but healthy children as well; not only children with green hair—but all children.

We owe the effort to ourselves. We were all kids once, and our elders gave us the world. Let us pass it on to a generation better than ours.

And let us remember that if there is shame in delinquency it belongs not to the delinquent but to ourselves, who created him in our own image.

THE END

www.ingramcontent.com/pod-product-compliance
Lightning Source LLC
Chambersburg PA
CBHW022356280326
41935CB00007B/202